Contents

p.06
What is Green Witchcraft?
Discover the environmental energy that surrounds us and how you can begin to embrace it

p.10
The Power of Earth
Earth encompasses both plants and the mineral magic of crystals

p.14
Creating an Earth Altar
How to create a sacred space to honour earth in your life

p.16
Go Barefoot
Deepen your connection to earth with this hands (and feet!) on ritual

p.18
Hello World
Learn how you can connect to the earth spirits of your local area

p.20
The Power of Sun
Sunlight provides the energy that makes everything grow

p.24
Creating a Sun Altar
How to create a sacred space to honour sunlight in your life

p.26
Catching some Rays
Enhance your connection to the sun's power by basking in its light

p.28
Let the Light In
Use the revealing power of sunlight to ritually cleanse your space

p.30
The Power of Water
Water is the hydrating force that nourishes life on earth

p.34
Creating a Water Altar
How to create a sacred space to honour water in your life

p.36
Go with the Flow
Connect with water and let its life-giving energy flow through you

p.38
Watering Can...
Discover water's ability to boost your energy and mood with this ritual

p.40
The Magic of Pollen
Explore the mystery and magic of this key part of life on Earth

p.44
Bathe in Beauty
Try this refreshing rose spell to amplify your powers of attraction

p.46
Plant Power
Discover some of the roles plants play in our lives and culture

p.50
Druid Tree Wisdom
Find out about the ancient and sacred knowledge of the trees

p.52
Embrace the Path of the Hedgewitch
Be inspired by green witchcraft's emphasis on the individual

p.56
Divine Inspiration
Learn about some of the earth deities and energies you might encounter

 **20**

 **70**

 **104**

p.62
The Wheel of the Year
Discover the modern Pagan calendar and its seasonal celebrations

p.64
Yule
Find out about the midwinter solstice festival of the returning sun

p.66
Imbolc
Explore the February festival of candlelight, sunlight and green shoots

p.68
Ostara
See how this festival of the spring equinox has some familiar folk imagery

p.70
Beltane
Explore this spring celebration of fire, feasting and fun

p.72
Litha
Discover the lore of the midsummer celebration of the summer solstice

p.74
Lughnasadh
Find out about the tales behind the first harvest festival of the year

p.76
Mabon
Learn about the rites and rituals of the autumn equinox

p.78
Samhain
Discover the ancient roots of Halloween in this festival of darkness and death

p.80
Seasons, Signs & Decans
Learn about the rhythms of the seasons and the signs of the zodiac

p.86
Gardening with the Moon
Discover how following the cycle of the moon can help your garden to flourish

p.92
The Witches Apothecary
Soothe your senses with some herbal healing knowledge

p.96
Kitchen Craft
Cook up some homemade magic with kitchen witchcraft

p.100
Hearty Party Punch
Try this kitchen-witch party popper to get shy guests mingling

p.102
Calm-down Cake
Bake this soothing teatime treat when relaxation is needed

p.104
Go Crazy for Crystals
Explore the magical, mystical powers of crystals and minerals

p.108
How Crystals Work
Get the lowdown on how crystals are thought to function

p.110
The Magic of Crystals
Discover which crystals are best for magical uses, and why

p.114
Grow your Garden with a Gemstone Grid
Set up this crystal spell to enhance your garden's green power

 **38**

Images Getty Images, Shutterstock, Alamy

What is Green Witchcraft?

IF YOU'RE DRAWN TO PLANTS AND TREES, HAVE EVER BEEN DESCRIBED AS GREEN-FINGERED, OR WANT TO FORGE A DEEPER CONNECTION WITH MOTHER NATURE, GREEN WITCHCRAFT IS FOR YOU

WORDS April Madden

Have you ever seen a plant growing straight out of the pavement? The force that drives nature is one of the strongest and most magical that we know of. Green growing things can push their way up through layers of concrete and pull apart buildings; left to its own devices nature can rewild a scrap of wasteland in just a few short seasons. Yet it can also be gentle and nourishing – green plants are the key building block of our food chain and provide many of our textiles.

Spending time in green space has been proven to calm feelings of stress and anxiety and help us to feel more stable and energised. The earliest modern humans we know about evolved in a lush, sundrenched, verdant riverside landscape. Perhaps it's that ancient connection that subconsciously informs the sense of contentment we experience in similar green spaces today.

That early habitat was abundant in the two key elements for plant growth – sunlight and water. These fuel the process of photosynthesis that allows plants to grow, creating oxygen, the essential element of the air we breathe, as a by-product. It's no exaggeration to say that without greenery, we wouldn't survive: it feeds us, clothes us, and supplies us with fresh air. The role of plants and trees in our ecosystem is the perfect demonstration of how everything in nature is interlinked and interdependent, and green witchcraft explores the mystical side of this deep, essential and ancient connection between every element of the world around us.

WHAT IS GREEN WITCHCRAFT?

> **Green witchcraft explores the mystical side of the deep connection between every element of the world around us**

Green witchcraft allows us to forge a deep and meaningful connection to the living world around us

WHY NOT TRY...
In Japan people are encouraged to practise shinrin-yoku, or forest-bathing. Simply spending time near trees is proven to reduce stress levels and encourage peace

Reap What You Sow

A powerful reminder of the circle of life and death – and a source of more plants for you!

A seed is a symbol of potential. Locked inside its tiny form is the energy and impetus to grow into a plant. But despite their truly magical nature, seeds don't just mysteriously spring up out of nowhere.

Plants produce seeds at the end of their life cycle. They will then either die completely (known as annuals) or fade back into the energy repository of their bulb, tuber or root, sleeping in the earth until it's time for them to begin anew (known as perennials). If your garden flowers are fading and going to seed, don't tidy away those dying stalks – let them do their thing and self-seed, or harvest and plant them so that you can have more blooms next year.

Your Own Space

You don't need a garden to be green!

Sometimes when we think of a 'green witch' we see someone who has access to a large amount of green space: their own garden or even rolling fields and woods. But you can be a green witch even if you live in a high-rise apartment in the middle of a city in the desert! The most important thing is to be able to forge a connection to that green life source that connects us to the rest of the planet, and you can do that with a houseplant or even a green crystal. Just make sure you have some quiet time in a clean, peaceful space to spend time with them and reflect. You can make just as valid and valuable a connection as someone with a garden full of plants and trees.

GREEN WITCHCRAFT

Get Started with Green Witchcraft

1 Pick up a plant

Take care of a houseplant and watch as it changes and grows. If you've never done this before, pothos are fast-growing and easy to look after.

2 Try crystal meditation

All crystals come from the Earth, but particularly good ones to meditate on green witchcraft with are sediment jasper, malachite and all shades of green stones.

3 Get out into nature

Find a green space to sit quietly and relax, whether that's a meadow or woodland or as simple as your local park.

A Planet-Focused Lifestyle

You don't have to be plant-based to be planet-focused

Natural foods and fabrics will always be better for us and the environment than heavily processed or synthetic ones, but many things you might think are environmentally friendly hide a hidden cost. We're regularly informed of the impact of meat and dairy farming on greenhouse gases, but did you know industrial almond farming has put an inordinate strain on some regions' water supplies and honey bees? Try to purchase the foods you eat from smaller and more local producers wherever possible.

Cotton and linen (flax) farming also have a huge impact on nearby water and wildlife, while semi-synthetics like bamboo fabric, lyocell and viscose use production processes that can lead to pollution. Look for sustainably sourced natural fabrics or the 'Ecovero' label on semi-synthetics, and either leather from the food farming industry if you eat meat, or Pinatex and other plant-based leather substitutes if you don't. Try to avoid synthetics where you can, and prioritise recycled polyester and plastics where you can't.

Remember that workers in both the food and fabric industries are often among the world's most economically disadvantaged; where possible buy from companies with fair trade policies and transparent supply chains.

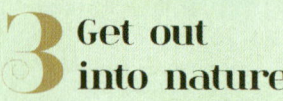

WHAT IS GREEN WITCHCRAFT?

> " Try to avoid synthetics where you can, and prioritise recycled polyester and plastics where you can't

When practising green witchcraft it's important to bring its philosophy of caring for the Earth into your daily life and consumption wherever you can

GREEN WITCHCRAFT

The Power of Earth

THE NURTURING, GROUND ELEMENT OF EARTH IS ONE THAT WE CAN ALL CONNECT WITH IN OUR DAILY LIVES, NO MATTER HOW HECTIC

WORDS Catherine Curzon

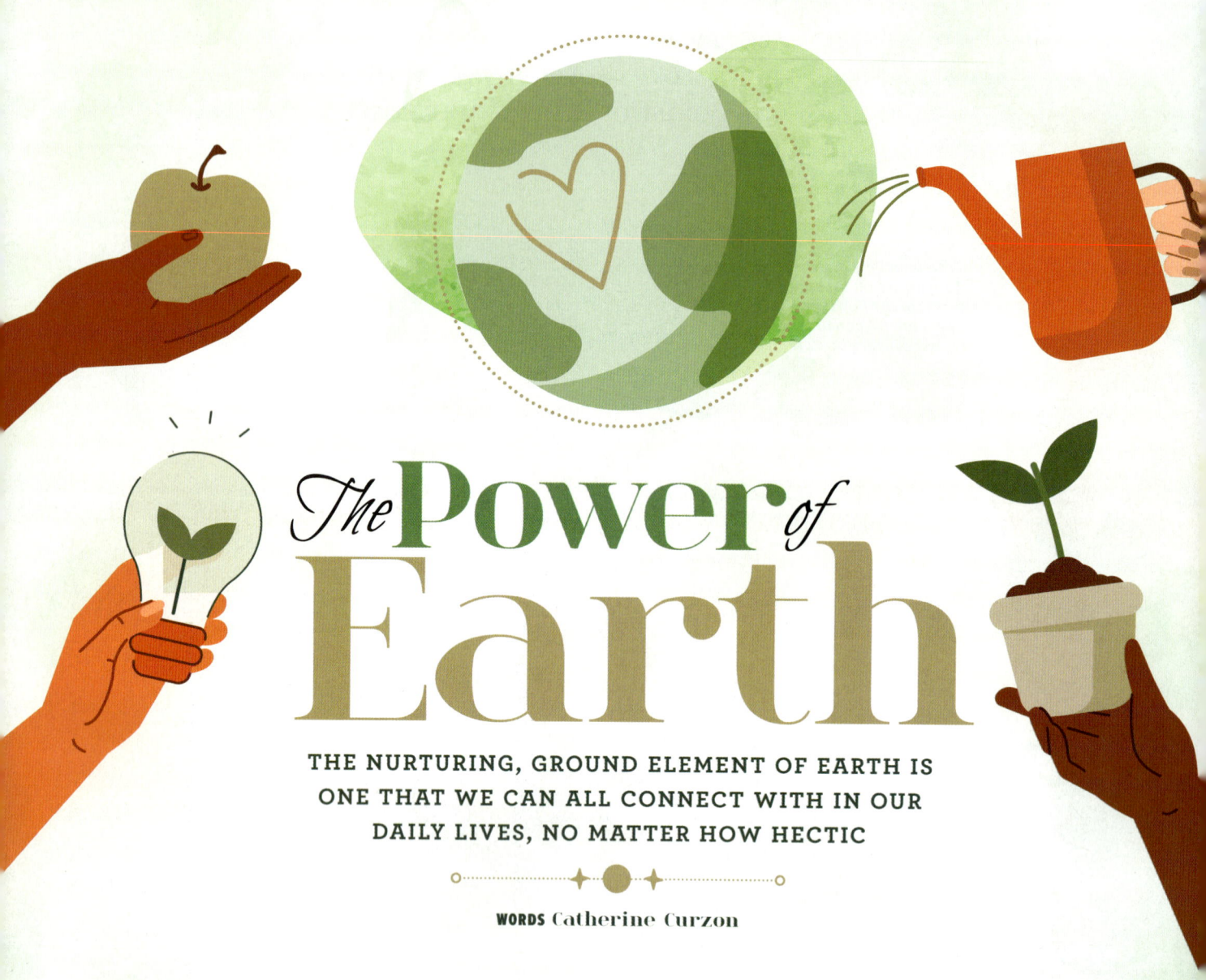

The modern world can sometimes seem chaotic and confusing, and it's all too easy to get swept along in the maelstrom of noise and activity. Before we know it, we've lost sight of anything but the here and now, reacting to the moment as it happens, and letting ourselves be overwhelmed by the sheer tumult of daily life.

Luckily, the earth element is always there, waiting for us to reconnect to it and regain a little balance and control in what can be a confusing world. Appropriately enough, the earth element and its rituals are all about grounding and balance, where the most simple action can carry its very own magic. The element of earth nurtures us and enfolds us, inviting us to remember all that is simple and natural and to feel that grounding force, binding us to the world around us.

When you work with the earth element, you're inviting good fortune and luck into your life and reminding yourself that, like everything in the world, you need nourishment too. There's little better nourishment for the soul than spending some time connecting with the earth, and silencing the concerns of the everyday for a little while.

> **The element of earth nurtures us and enfolds us, inviting us to remember all that is simple and natural**

THE POWER OF EARTH

WHY NOT TRY...
For a quick reconnection to the earth, simply sit quietly for a couple of minutes. It's an easy way to recentre yourself when things get loud

Blossoms & Blooms

Plants are a mindful and attractive pathway to connect with the earth

It will come as no surprise to learn that plants are one particularly mindful way to work with the earth element. Plants are nurtured by the very soil itself, so are a tangible and physical manifestation of the strength of the earth, and spending some time tending or simply being amongst plants and trees will give you a powerful boost of earth magic. And you don't have to be an expert – novice gardeners are just as welcome.

The Power of Earth

Like all of the elements, the earth has its own very unique strengths

Each of the four elements has its own very unique strength and associations, and when it comes to the earth element, the keywords are nurture and growth.
Just as the earth itself nurtures animal and plant life and plays a vital part in the cycle of renewal, the earth element is linked closely to those same qualities.

The element of earth is one of stability and safety, of nurture and, ultimately, growth. Just as a humble acorn can grow into a towering oak tree, when you incorporate the earth element in your practice, your own potential for growth will be limitless.

This harmonious and benevolent element doesn't need a lot of show and drama, its secrets lie in its very humble nature. It reveals the beauty in simplicity and sometimes, in that simplicity, you might find you discover the greatest fortunes of all.

DID YOU KNOW...
Earth is the element that keeps us in balance. When life seems chaotic, connecting to the earth will bring some much-needed harmony

THE POWER OF EARTH

Working with Crystals

Crystals offer a fantastic way to connect with the earth

Crystals offer a wonderful way to connect with the earth element. By incorporating earth element crystals such as black agate, green jade or red tiger's eye into your everyday life, you can benefit from crystal energy all day long. Whether you choose to wear them as jewellery, create your own crystal grids, or simply pop them on your desk or in a pocket, they'll bring the power of the earth element into every aspect of your life.

Connect with Earth

1 Escape the Daily Grind

Spend a day completely connected to the earth. Leave your phone at home, find a secluded spot, and allow yourself to just be.

2 Make the Earth Everyday

Take half an hour for yourself and enjoy a walk in a local park or green space, where you can enjoy the simplicity around you.

3 Bring the Earth Home

Grow a favourite plant or herb on your windowsill from seed. As you nurture your new project, you'll truly welcome the earth element into your home.

❝ The element of earth is one of stability and safety, of nurture and, ultimately, growth

Images Getty Images

13

GREEN WITCHCRAFT

Creating an Earth Altar

AN EARTH ALTAR IS THE PLACE WHERE PLANES MEET;
USING NATURAL ELEMENTS, THEY OFFER THE CHANCE
TO CONNECT THE SPIRITUAL AND THE PHYSICAL

WORDS Catherine Curzon

Creating an earth altar offers a wonderful opportunity to tap into something far bigger than ourselves. By gathering found materials and setting positive, clear intentions, the act of creating the altar will allow you to truly leave the everyday behind and connect to the larger cosmos. Best of all, creating an earth altar is something anyone can do; it will be your creation and a unique expression of your own relationship with the earth.

CREATING AN EARTH ALTAR

1 Consider Your Altar
Before you start, spend some time thinking about the work you're about to undertake and why. Consider generations who have gone before, with whom you will now make your own connection.

2 Set Your Intention
Think about why you want to build the altar and what you hope to achieve when you work with it. Do you wish to connect with yourself, your ancestors or something else? It's okay to be vague, this is your special space.

3 Gather Your Materials
Now you can go out and let the earth guide you as you gather whatever materials appeal to you. Only gather what the earth offers in plentiful supply, whether it's from your garden, the beach, woodland or further afield.

4 Create the Altar
How you create the altar is up to you. You might choose to build a cairn of rocks, lay out a mandala or even make tree decorations. You could also gather the items you've collected together, focusing on your intentions as you let your hands guide you.

5 Connect with Your Altar
Now you've made your altar, it is time to use it. Sit before your altar and focus on connecting with it, imagining the energy that connects you to the wider cosmos. You've created this sacred space for yourself, so enjoy that connection and all that it brings.

You'll Need...
- A basket, bag or other receptacle
- Clippers
- Pebbles
- Shells
- Pine cones
- Leaves
- Petals
- Rocks
- Flowers
- Twigs
- Anything the earth offers up!

GREEN WITCHCRAFT

Go Barefoot

CONNECTING TO NATURE AND OPENING YOUR MIND TO THE POWERS OF THE NATURAL WORLD CAN BE AS SIMPLE AS SLIPPING OFF YOUR SHOES

WORDS Ben Gazur

Study after study has shown that spending time in nature is good for our mental health. Just a few hours among plants reduces anxiety and stress, as well as improving your mood. One of the easiest ways you get a natural boost is to kick off your shoes and socks and stand barefoot on the grass. As well as the proven benefits of being in nature, you will be transported back to your childhood, when running about with bare feet was a mark of your freedom from worry.

Going barefoot offers wonderful new vistas for mindfulness. The nerves on our feet are incredibly sensitive and wearing shoes can dull us to a whole world beneath us. Allowing ourselves to feel the grass, earth, or sand creates a feeling of connection to the world that might otherwise be lacking. Some practitioners refer to going barefoot as earthing or grounding because of the link that forms between the person and the Earth.

To begin your meditation, find a spot outdoors where you can focus without too many distractions. Make sure the ground is free from rubbish (particularly broken glass), dog mess and any particularly pointy pebbles. Take off your shoes and socks so that there is nothing coming between you and the ground. Plant your feet a comfortable distance apart and parallel to each other. Flex your toes and bring each one down to the ground in turn. Notice the sensations that well up from this contact. For those who are unable to stand, another approach is to lay on the ground and allow your fingertips to explore the earth under you. Place your fingertips firmly down and sense the connection they form.

Now breath deeply. As you open your lungs imagine that you are pulling energy from the Earth. Feel it travelling up through your exposed skin in contact with the ground and upwards until it suffuses your entire body. As you exhale, picture the energy emerging from you like a plume. Repeat this three times then relax and clear your mind.

If you cannot go to a quiet space outdoors, then houseplants offer the convenience of connecting with nature in your own home. Make sure your plant is a not a skin-irritating species. Sit comfortably in front of it. Notice as much detail as you can. Then close your eyes and allow your fingers to wander over the leaves and stalks. What do you notice that your eyes may have missed? Now try the breathing exercise above as you focus on the connection you have made with your plant.

WHY NOT TRY...
If you have mobility issues or don't want to go barefoot, a meaningful connection can be made by touching plants – even in your own home

GO BAREFOOT

" Going barefoot offers wonderful new vistas for mindfulness

GREEN WITCHCRAFT

Hello World

EXPAND YOUR CONSCIOUSNESS OUTWARDS AND LEARN HOW TO GREET AND EMBRACE THE SPIRIT OF A PLACE

WORDS April Madden

Have you ever felt that some places have a distinct presence? A personality of their own? In green witchcraft we learn to reach out to these spirits of place and greet them as potential friends and allies.

In the ancient pagan religion of classical Rome, a genius loci was the spirit of a place. Not quite a god but definitely not human, these spirits were honoured by locals and passersby, and in return it was believed that they protected their woodlands, or enriched their fields, or purified their water – whatever it was the genius loci watched over. Many other folk traditions had similar concepts, such as the Slavic leshy. Modern witchcraft often borrows the Sanskrit word 'deva' from ancient Hindu and Zoroastrian beliefs, and uses it to refer to these guardians, extending it to other nature spirits like that of a particularly old and potent tree.

To connect with a deva or genius loci, start small and local, in a nearby park or even your garden. If it's a

 **In the ancient religion of classical Rome, a genius loci was the spirit of a place and honoured by locals**

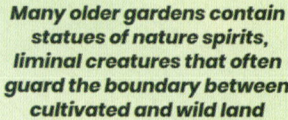

Many older gardens contain statues of nature spirits, liminal creatures that often guard the boundary between cultivated and wild land

18

HELLO WORLD

Your local area is a microcosm of Earth, with areas of green space, water, hot and cold, field and fallow. Go exploring!

You'll Need...

- Clothing and shoes suitable for the place you're going
- Your phone, fully charged
- A snack or picnic and a drink
- A map, if necessary
- An emergency first aid kit, if necessary
- A rubbish bag

place you pass regularly, chances are its local nature spirits will already be aware of you. Sit or stand in your chosen place and say (aloud, or in your mind if you prefer) "Hail, old one; I greet you in my name and yours." Sit and have your snack or picnic and drink, making sure to offer some of the crumbs and a libation of the liquid to the spirit of the place and the wildlife that it protects. You are sharing dinner with a potential new friend; meditate on what the conversation might be. Remember to clean up after yourself! You need to show your new friend you are respectful of its home.

If you choose to journey further afield and into wild places, make sure you are correctly equipped – your destination will have a website that lists the proper equipment needed, such as hiking boots, how much water you should bring, and safety measures. Make sure your phone is on and charged, and that you tell people where you're going and when you expect to be back. But you don't need to climb mountains; green witchcraft is all about being aware of the land you live on. Get to know it!

You don't have to go far to encounter a nature spirit – one of the best places to go is your local park

ALTERNATIVELY

If you find it difficult to get outdoors, sit by a window and focus on a tree that you can see, or ask someone to bring you a pebble from a local green space to hold

GREEN WITCHCRAFT

The Power of Sun

THE SUN'S ENERGY IS ESSENTIAL TO GREEN MAGIC. IT POWERS THE PROCESS OF PHOTOSYNTHESIS AND BRINGS LIFE TO THE EARTH

WORDS Poppy-Jay St Palmer

You probably remember this from school: Photosynthesis is the process by which plants' growth and lifecycle is fuelled. Take that out of the classroom and stop and think for a moment how magical it is – plants grow and transform themselves using the power of sunlight. A side effect of that process is the creation of oxygen, the essential element of the air we breathe. In green magic, sun is the power of energy, of awakening, growth and transformation, and together with earth and water it's one of the three key elements of green magic.

WHY NOT TRY...

Charge your magical tools or crystals when the sun is at its peak at noon. Note that some types of crystals fade in the sunlight, so check before you leave them out to charge!

THE POWER OF SUN

Sun Salutation

Greet the sun with this sequence of yoga moves

In yoga, the Sun Salutation is used to both warm up the spine and improve the body's energy. The 12-posture sequence involves flowing movements that come together for an entire body stretch that counterbalances the bending of the spine and opens the heart, shoulders and chest. Traditionally, the Sun Salutation is practised while facing east at sunrise or west at sunset and focuses on pranayama (breathwork), asana (movement), mantra (chanting) and chakra (energy centre) awareness.

> "Just like the moon, different phases of the sun possess different magical properties"

Sunrise, Sunset

Sun phases and their magical properties

Just like the moon, different phases of the sun possess different magical properties that can be used in a number of spells and rituals. The sunrise represents new beginnings, renewal and changes, as well as health, employment, resurrection and finding the right direction. As the morning sun gains strength, it's all about growth, positive energy, courage, harmony, happiness, projects and plans, prosperity and the expansion of ideas. The sun at high noon is good for magic involving health, physical energy, wisdom and knowledge. The sun's descent in the afternoon is connected to positive professional matters, communication, clarity, travel and exploration. Finally, sunset represents all magic relating to removing depression, stress and confusion, letting go, and finding out the truth of a situation. To make the most of the sun's power, perform spells and rituals at different times of day depending on what you want to get out of them.

Let the Sun Shine

Harness the magical properties of the sun

As our solar system's biggest star, the sun contains multitudes of magical properties. Whether your intent is to bring about professional success or to inspire joy and freedom, the sun can be used in many different spells and rituals. The following are some areas of intent where the sun will prove itself to be very useful: success, empowerment, ambition, goals, generosity, spirituality, male energy, health, vitality, the Gods, joy, freedom, leadership, matters of the heart, creativity, friendship, growth, personal fulfilment, self-confidence, wealth, individuality, pride, energy and power.

You could get started by trying the following releasing spell at sunset:

1 Set out four lit candles.

2 Briefly write down on four small pieces of paper what you'd like to release.

3 Use each candle to set fire to each piece of paper and leave them to burn safely in a fireproof dish.

4 Snuff out each candle in reverse order.

5 Look towards the sun as it goes down beyond the horizon and say: "The end of my woes, ready for the beginning of a new day".

GREEN WITCHCRAFT

Sunwise *and* Widdershins

 Take the path of the sun

Themes of the sun have long been featured in folklore from around the world. In Scottish folklore, turning from east to west in a clockwise direction was believed to be prosperous because it was the same route taken by the sun. The direction became known as 'sunwise'. It is believed that the druids would walk around their temples sunwise to bring about good fortune. The opposite direction was known as widdershins, and was considered unprosperous at best and sometimes even fatal.

Sun Safety

Be smart in direct sunlight

Although the sun can be very healing, having too much of it can also be bad for your health, including increasing your risk of developing skin cancer. When enjoying solar power, please act responsibly. Here are a few things to remember:

- Spend time in the shade in the summertime when the sun is at its most powerful.

- Always wear sunscreen when in direct sunlight, with SPF of at least 30 to protect against UVB, even if you don't usually burn. Keep applying the sunscreen throughout the day, especially if your summer rituals involve water, as it will wash off.

- Direct sunlight can damage your eyes without proper protection, so always carry a good pair of sunglasses with you. Never look directly at the sun or a solar eclipse.

- Don't expose your skin to direct sunlight for too long. A little bit here and there will give you a nice dose of vitamin D, but cover up with cool, flowing clothes and a hat.

WHY NOT TRY...
Celebrate the spring equinox with a random act of kindness, like donating to a worthy cause or offering someone in need a helping hand. These good deeds create energy flow

THE Power of sun

Solar Power

Try these rituals to harness the power of the sun and improve your mood:

MAKE YOUR OWN SUN WATER Fill a glass jar with water and leave it in the sun so it can absorb the natural light. You can also mix in some ingredients associated with the sun, like a few drops of lemon essential oil or a handful of sunflower petals.

BREW LEMON TEA As lemon is a powerful sun symbol, lemon tea is the perfect concoction to capture the sun's solar energy. Once brewed, you can offer some of the tea near the roots of an old tree while reciting affirmations.

ENJOY A CITRUS BATH Harness the sun's magic while you bathe and relax by running a cool water bath after an afternoon spent in the sun. You might want to add some orange slices, flowers, citrus oils or maybe even champagne!

CHARGE YOUR CRYSTALS Leave your crystals and other tools out in the sun to charge using the sun's energy.

Sun Worship

How to put together your first sun altar

Harness the power of the sun by performing spells and rituals at a homemade sun altar. Magical altars are very personal and each person's sun altar will be unique, but here are a few suggestions to get you started:

- Flowers in yellows, oranges and reds to match the sun's phases.
- Fruit, like pieces of orange and lemon.
- Knick-knacks featuring sun symbols, like scarves, mirrors, and jewellery.
- Candles in fiery colours.

Solstices & Equinoxes

A celebration of the seasons

The changing of seasons can bring about many different emotions. But whether we're moving towards the light or the dark it can feel very healing to celebrate the passing of time. The equinox happens twice each year, and marks the time at which the sun crosses the equator's path and becomes positioned directly above the equator between the Northern and Southern Hemispheres. In the Northern Hemisphere, the spring equinox occurs around 20 March while the autumn equinox happens around 22 September. The dates are reversed in the Southern Hemisphere. The word 'equinox' is derived from the Latin equi meaning 'equal' and nox meaning 'night' – around this time, day and night become the same length as we welcome in a new season. The solstices occur on 21 June and 21 December, when the sun reaches its highest and lowest points in the sky. The summer solstice is often seen as a time for celebration as we reach the longest day of the year, the day with the most sunlight. There are many different ways to enjoy the summer solstice, from mediating and sunbathing to observing the sunrise and sunset. Winter solstices are the opposite, the shortest day of the year and a time of darkness. However, many people like to embrace the dark by performing rituals by candlelight and releasing any negative feelings they were holding as they welcome the fact that the days will finally begin to get longer.

Images Getty Images

GREEN WITCHCRAFT

Creating a Sun Altar

THE WARMTH, HEAT AND VITALITY OF THE SUN IS JUST WAITING TO CONNECT WITH YOU, AND AN ALTAR OFFERS A GREAT WAY TO DO IT

WORDS Catherine Curzon

The sun is the bringer of life, light and warmth; it's a symbol of passion and fire and strength. By building an altar to the sun, you can work with its power and harness your own inner fire, letting it light every corner of your inner self and your outer life. It's little wonder that our ancient ancestors have looked to the sun for centuries, and that we continue to do so today.

CREATING A SUN ALTAR

1 Choose Your Space
If possible, an outdoor space is the perfect spot for your sun altar. If not, try to build it indoors in a place where it can get plenty of sunlight. Remember, it doesn't have to be huge.

2 Focus on Your Needs
The sun is all about rebirth and renewal, whilst its fire can cleanse, empower and fortify. Focus on what you want to use the power of the sun for as you prepare to gather your items. If it helps, write down your intention.

3 Gather Your Items
You can include anything that speaks to you on your altar, but items in colours such as red, orange and gold are ideal. Be sure to include plenty of lights, from fiery lights to candles, but take care when working with flames.

4 Build Your Altar
Whether indoors or out, let your imagination run wild when you build your altar. Make it as elaborate or simple as you wish, and make it a real place of celebration and connection to the universe.

5 Use Your Altar
Take your time to work with and meditate before your altar. If you wrote down your intention down, burn the paper in the candle flame to bind it to the sun's power. Never leave candles unattended – stay safe and enjoy your connection!

You'll Need...

- Candles
- Matches or lighter
- A receptacle for the items
- Items that speak to you of sun – reds, oranges and gold
- Lights
- Flowers
- Images representing the sun
- Something to extinguish the flame
- A place in the sun

GREEN WITCHCRAFT

Catching *some* Rays

WE'VE ALL ENJOYED THE SUN'S WARMTH, AND IT OFFERS THE PERFECT ELEMENT FOR AN EMPOWERING, INVIGORATING MEDITATION

WORDS Catherine Curzon

The sun's warmth, strength and light is vital to life on Earth. It gives us and the world around us energy, from the most humble plant to the largest creature, and by bringing its power into meditative practices, we can benefit from its unique properties. Just as even the smallest plants are able to absorb the sun's light and turn it into energy via photosynthesis, so are we able to harness it for our own growth, both physical and spiritual.

> The sun's warmth, strength and light is vital to life on Earth

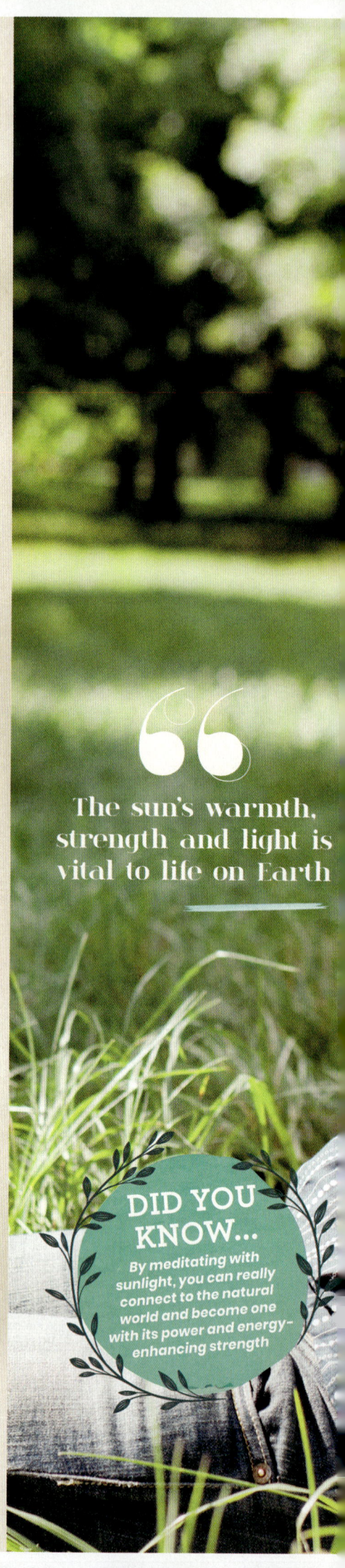

DID YOU KNOW...
By meditating with sunlight, you can really connect to the natural world and become one with its power and energy-enhancing strength

CATCHING SOME RAYS

Start with Sun Safety

Meditating outdoors in the sun is in itself a powerful and rewarding experience, offering as it does a unique opportunity to exist as part of the natural world, free of the cares of the everyday. However, before you find a peaceful spot in the sun or shade, remember to take sensible precautions. Pop on a hat and some sunscreen, so your time in the sun remains a positive one. If you can't find a suitable outdoor space, then find somewhere indoors where you can see and feel the sun. Beside a window is perfect, and of course this mediation must be practiced in the daytime!

Meditation

Settle into a comfortable position for meditation and close your eyes. As you settle into your meditation, focus on the very top of your head, and feel the warmth of the sun's light entering through your head as it begins to fill your body. Really envision the light and heat of the rays of the sun as they bathe your head and shoulders; if you're in the sun this should be a literal process but if you prefer a shady spot, simply remember that sense of wellbeing and warmth, which we have all felt in our lives. As you welcome the warming light of the sun, visualise your entire body filling with the energy-giving rays, and imagine yourself bathed in a bright, golden sunlight, so strong that it shines out of your every pore. Picture that light as the source of your own empowering energy, just as a plant is able to do via photosynthesis, and enjoy sharing in that natural process. Stay in your meditation for as long as you wish, and when you are ready to return to the conscious world, do so slowly and in your own time, bringing the strength and energy of the sun with you as you resume your day.

GREEN WITCHCRAFT

Let the Light In

SUNSHINE'S ASSOCIATION WITH SPRING CLEANING MAKES IT THE PERFECT COMPANION TO HELP YOU CLEANSE AND BRIGHTEN YOUR SPACE

WORDS April Madden

There's a reason why people traditionally give their houses a deep clean in spring. In a time when you had to move your possessions outside to clean them properly, the longer, drier, warmer days made it more practical to roll up your sleeves and get scrubbing. Meanwhile the brighter sunshine of the season lit up dark corners, and was also useful for drying and bleaching textiles. Today we don't need to factor these things into our cleaning rota, and we have a lot of helpful tools that mean we can keep our homes clean all year round, but we still reflexively refer to 'spring cleaning' as something that brings light and energy into a space. Happily, these days you don't need to wait for the turn of the year to bring some of that invigorating energy into your home. All you need is a bright sunny day when you can open the windows wide and get the dust – real or symbolic – moving.

Start by filling your spray bottle with some sun water that you've made earlier. If you wish, you can pop a smooth citrine tumblestone in there too. Next, grab your broom or duster and start sweeping your space in an anticlockwise direction. Anticlockwise, or widdershins, is the direction we move things in when we want them to go away. As you sweep or dust, focus on pushing out any negative energy. Visualise the warm light of the sun poking into the dark and shadowy corners of both your home and your mind and helping you light up and disperse the dust and rubbish you find.

When you're done with sweeping or dusting, spray your sun water around the room in a clockwise direction – this has the practical advantage of damping down any remaining dust as well as blessing your space with the cleansing energy of sunlight. We go clockwise, or sunwise, when we want to invite

Citrine's cheerful sunlit appearance and ability to absorb negative energy and convert it into good vibes make it an ideal cleansing crystal

LET THE LIGHT IN

Lemons' bright vivid scent and colour associates them with the sun, but their astringent properties also make them great for cutting through dirt!

You'll Need...

- Lemon scented candle (or plain yellow candle anointed with lemon essential oil)
- Duster or broom
- A bright sunny day
- Sun water (see p34) in a spray bottle
- Citrine crystal (optional)

something in. If you chose to put a citrine crystal in your spray bottle, take it out when you're done and dry it off. You may want to quickly finish off any cleaning with a cloth or vacuum.

Light your lemon candle and visualise yourself and your space filling with the warm, golden, friendly light of the sun. If you used a citrine crystal, place it in a corner of the room. Citrine has the ability to take negative energy and transform it into positive, sunlit vibes. Beware of putting your citrine in direct sunlight though – this yellow quartz is so fond of the sun that it can leach out all of its colour!

WARNING

If you have asthma, allergies or other breathing difficulties, make sure to take an antihistamine beforehand or even wear a cloth face mask while dusting if you need to. You could also use a mini vacuum cleaner!

GREEN WITCHCRAFT

The Power of Water

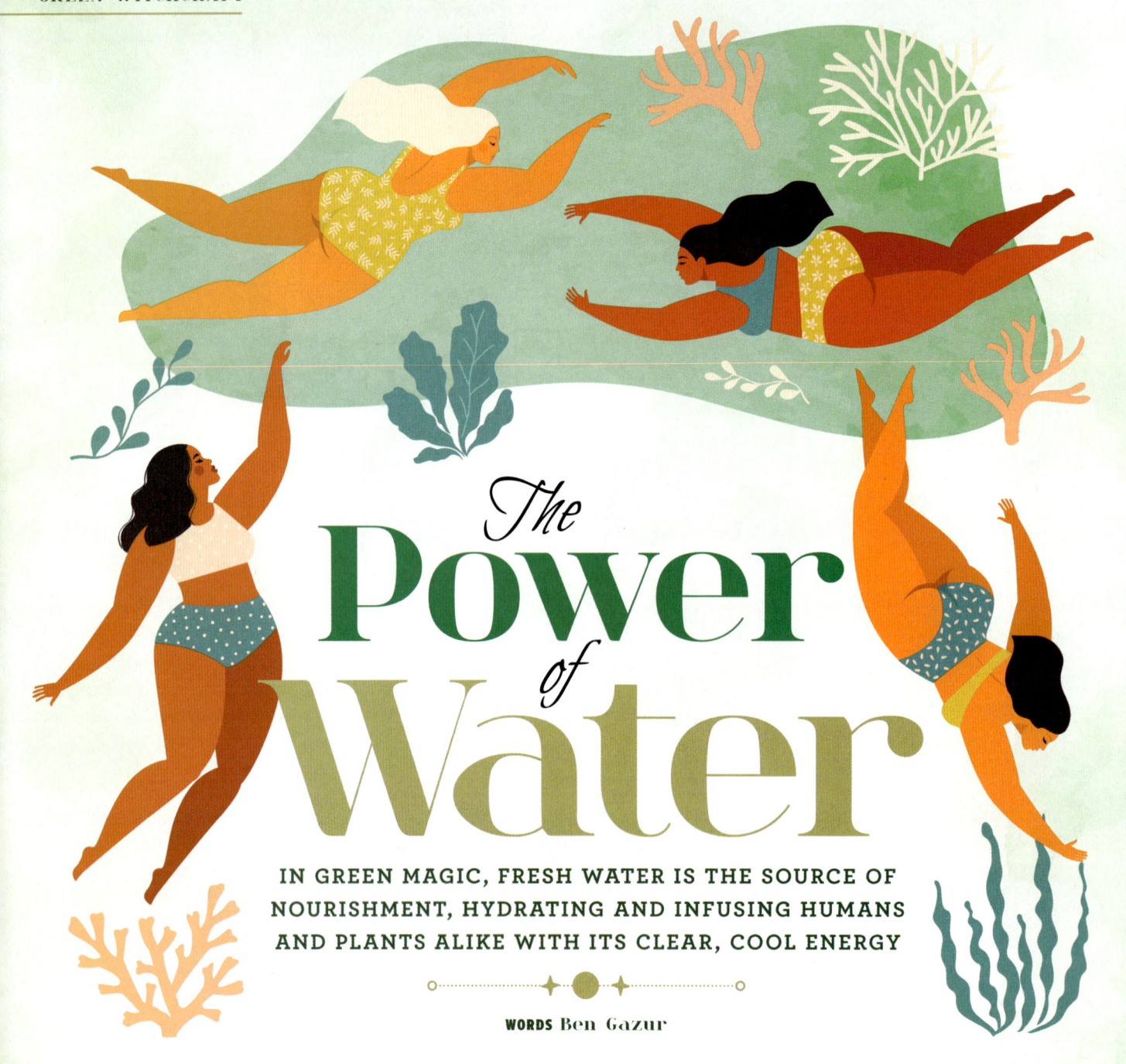

IN GREEN MAGIC, FRESH WATER IS THE SOURCE OF NOURISHMENT, HYDRATING AND INFUSING HUMANS AND PLANTS ALIKE WITH ITS CLEAR, COOL ENERGY

WORDS Ben Gazur

Water is vital to life. Life itself evolved in water. Many cultures have seen water as central to their religious and spiritual rites. In green magic, water's quenching energy is vital to plant growth. Along with earth and sun it's part of the process of photosynthesis. It also nourishes and swells a plant's cells and kickstarts the germination of seeds.

Because we all need water every day to be healthy, it can be easy to overlook its qualities. When we need to be clean we turn to water and either submerge ourselves in a bath

> By reflecting on the nature of water and using it in mindfulness practices we can all find ways to still our minds

or wash ourselves in a shower. This purifying power of water on the body is reflected in its effects on the soul. Ritual purity in religion often comes from contact with specially blessed water.

All water is special however. The power of water can be seen in its ability to be many things and yet remain essentially itself. Whether it is a running river, an ocean wave, a cloud, or a falling snowflake, water can always return to itself. In green magic we mainly focus on fresh water, but there are a range of plants, known as halophytes, that thrive on seawater.

THE POWER OF WATER

DID YOU KNOW?
Misogi is a Shinto practice where worshippers become ritually pure by chanting and then standing under sacred waterfalls

The Clarity of Water

The transparency of water reflects its purity

When water is perfectly pure it has a crystal clear appearance. Sometimes you stumble on a body of water where it is so clear that it can be hard to tell there is any water there at all. Yet when you place an object in water it can appear to be distorted or bent due to the natural refractive properties of water. By considering how even the clearest image can be deceiving we reconsider all we think we know.

GREEN WITCHCRAFT

> "Today water is most often thought of as a soothing element. The stress of the day is washed away in water"

The Meanings of Water

The symbolism of water is as liquid as water itself

Across history and cultures water has been symbolic of a myriad of concepts. It can mean cohesion, as when droplets merge together, or chaos, as when a storm churns up the ocean. In fact many mythologies pictured the state of chaos before the creation of the world by representing it as water. Water can be the softly flowing stream that brings life and fertility or it can be the relentless dripping that will eventually wear away the strongest stone.

Today water is most often thought of as a soothing element which relaxes the body and calms the mind. The stress of the day is washed away in water and it refreshes and invigorates us. For centuries people have travelled to special bodies of water in hopes of healing their illnesses and the image of water as a relief from pain is a powerful one.

DID YOU KNOW...
The meanings of water are as changeable as the forms it can take

THE POWER OF WATER

Washing in Water

Cleanliness is next to godliness

Clean water is essential to all humans. Not only do we drink it, we wash in it. For thousands of years people have taken baths for their health whether in rivers, ponds, hot springs, or Roman bath houses. It is not only bodily purity that water has offered however. Before many religious ceremonies water was used to remove any spiritual dirt clinging to a person. Water was thought able to carry both away and leave a person clean.

Connect with Water

1 Embrace the rain

A rainy day may be dull for us, but our gardens love it. Step out into the refreshing summer rain and feel what they do!

2 Relax in the bath

Submerge yourself in a warm bath and feel how each part of your body reacts to the embrace of the water.

3 Make waves

Take a bowl of water and touch the surface, allow drips to fall from your finger, and follow the patterns of ripples that form.

 **Water was used before many religious ceremonies to remove any spiritual dirt clinging to a person**

Images Getty Images

GREEN WITCHCRAFT

Creating a Water Altar

THE ELEMENT OF WATER OFFERS A CLEANSING, SPIRITUAL MEDIUM TO WORK WITH. YOU CAN HARNESS ITS POWER WITH AN ALTAR

WORDS Catherine Curzon

Creating a water altar doesn't have to mean involving a huge body of water, nor access to the ocean or another natural water source. It can be as elaborate or simple as your needs and space dictates, because as with all spiritual matters, it's the intention that counts. Taking time to connect your spiritual self with the cleansing and purifying power of water will open up a whole new realm of awareness and connection.

CREATING A WATER ALTAR

1 Set Your Intention
Think about where to place your altar and what you hope to achieve. The element of water is a powerful one for cleansing and healing, and for bringing life, peace and transformation.

2 Gather Your Items
Listen to your intuition as you gather offerings to place on your altar. Though seashells and the like are obvious choices, anything that speaks to you as belonging should be included. Don't forget to add some water too!

3 Charge Your Water
If you want to imbue your water offering with the power of the moon or sun, then this is the time to charge it. Place a container of water in the window overnight or throughout the day, to let it soak up the powerful rays.

4 Set Up Your Altar
When it comes to setting up your altar, let your imagination guide you. There are no right or wrong answers, it's all about what works for you. If it feels right, it will be right.

5 Bask in Your Work
Once your altar is complete, you can use it in your meditative or other practice. You can add and replenish items as you need, and be sure to keep the water refreshed and charged for maximum power.

You'll Need...
- A container for water
- Some water to put in the container – from a natural source if possible
- A bag or other receptacle
- Any object that you associate with water, for example:
- Shells
- Pebbles
- Blue crystals
- Ornaments of water-dwelling creatures like fish or frogs

GREEN WITCHCRAFT

Go with the Flow

WATER IS A POTENT IMAGE FOR MEDITATION AND CAN BE EMPLOYED AT ANY TIME TO HELP CLEAR THE MIND OF TROUBLES AND THOUGHTS

WORDS Ben Gazur

Water has long been used in many religions as a means of cleansing oneself and bringing us to a state of purity. During meditation we can use the image of water for a similar purpose. The unending flow of water allows us to wash away many of the blockages in our mind and reveal what truly matters.

The beauty of water is that it comes in many forms. We can picture a still mountain lake that reflects nothing but the clear sky. We might think of a country pond surrounded by lush life. Water can be a gently burbling stream or a relentless tide moving in and out. It can even be a weightless cloud floating free. Each of these images might be helpful for us at different points in our life.

Water meditation can be performed in numerous ways. Some like to sit on the seashore or beside a body of water. Others prefer to submerge themselves in water while they meditate. Still others find even a comfortable bath is sufficient to connect with water. In truth, you can focus your mind on a cup of water or simply use your imagination.

However you connect with water, it is important to be free of distractions that might pull your mind out of focus. Get comfortable however feels best to you. Prepare yourself by noticing your thoughts. If one comes to your mind then allow it to flow away like water without making any lasting impression. Using the image of water, begin a breathing process. Inhale deeply and hold for several seconds before allowing the breath to slowly exhale. Repeat this until you no longer need to focus on your actions. Without effort, bring the image of water you want into being. Notice the state of the water and the situation around it. Feel the flow of the water and its relation to your emotional being.

Once the water is held in your mind, imagine submerging yourself into it. If the water is flowing, think of how its energy is entering you before being carried gently away. If the water is still then feel the perfect connection between your form and the liquid. Dissolve the boundaries between yourself and the water.

When you feel perfectly relaxed begin to focus again on your breathing. Bring your mind back into your body by making note of the sensations you are feeling. Let the image of water go as you gently end the meditation.

DID YOU KNOW...
You can use almost any body of water to help focus the mind – explore what each image may help you to discover

36

GO WITH THE FLOW

"The image of flowing water is an ideal metaphor for the carrying away the thoughts that bubble up in the mind

The ebb and flow of the tide connects us to the natural rhythms of the world and our own bodies

GREEN WITCHCRAFT

Watering Can...

This spell is an example of sympathetic magic, where we imitate the life-giving power of rain on plants to bring energy and growth into our own life

TAP INTO THE CAN-DO ENERGY
PLANTS EXPRESS WHEN THEY MEET
THE LIFE-GIVING POWER OF RAIN

WORDS April Madden

WATERING CAN...

Have you ever seen how plants put on a spurt of growth after a summer rainfall? If you feel tired or like you're having a creative drought and need a little of this get-up-and-go energy in your life, this simple, splashy ritual can help you to manifest it. If you're performing it outside, you'll want a warm day and some old clothes you don't mind getting a little wet. If you're indoors, use the draining board, sink, shower or bathtub to avoid splashing water around your home. It's best to do this spell in the morning or evening out of direct sunlight – while watering in bright sunlight won't actually scorch your plants, the soil will absorb more water in cooler, less bright conditions.

If you're using a candle or incense to help evoke the scent and feeling of rain, start by lighting that. Then take the blue bowl and fill it with water. Ask the water in the bowl to remember the last time it was rain, and the plants and trees it nurtured on its journey through earth and sky. Hold the pebble in your non-dominant hand and think about how the dry earth is transformed when rain falls on it.

When you're ready, fill your watering can or jug with the water from the bowl. Take the pebble and place it in your houseplant's pot, or among the outdoor plants you're going to water. Take the watering can. If you're using a jug instead, or your watering can doesn't have a rose (the round nozzle full of holes on the end of the spout), you'll need a sieve or tea strainer in your other hand to pour the water through. Say (aloud or in your head):

Rain, rain, quench and nourish
On the green earth all things flourish

And pour the water gently, swishing from side to side, to imitate slow summer rain. Focus on the soft, gentle fall of the water – notice how it splashes onto and slowly wets the pebble you held earlier – and inhale the scent of wet earth, stone and leaves. Welcome the feeling of calm but lively energy the 'rain' creates.

As you perform this ritual, meditate on the water cycle and what it teaches us about the interconnectedness of life on Earth

You'll Need...

- A blue bowl
- Fresh water
- A watering can or jug
- A kitchen sieve or tea strainer (optional)
- A garden or houseplant
- A pebble
- A rainfall or petrichor scented candle or incense (optional)

> *If you need a little get-up-and-go energy in your life, this simple ritual can help*

This ritual uses a blue bowl to symbolise fresh water in its purest and most nourishing state

WHY NOT TRY...
If you have a garden water butt to collect runoff, try using real rainwater in this ritual

Images Alamy

GREEN WITCHCRAFT

The Magic of Pollen

IN GREEN MAGIC, POLLINATION IS AN IMPORTANT PROCESS THAT INFORMS RITUAL, FOLKLORE AND THE VERY CYCLE OF LIFE ITSELF

WORDS Catherine Curzon

Pollination is nature's way of keeping the flowers in bloom, innumerable crops growing and the Earth's flora reproducing. Plants pollinate by self-pollination or cross-pollination, the first coming when pollen grains from the anther of a plant fall directly onto the stigma of the same type of plant. Cross-pollination, meanwhile, sees pollen transfer from one plant to another, whether by wind, water or with the help of animal and insect pollinators. Though we're all aware of the role of bumble bees in plant reproduction, they're only one part of a complex and amazing ecosystem.

Throughout history, practitioners of green magic have enjoyed a connection to the Earth and the natural world, open to the changing of the seasons and the natural processes of the Earth. Whilst seeking to understand and be in harmony with the planet, green magic practitioners today are still able to follow in the footsteps of their ancestors and bring the natural process of pollination into their rituals and practices. You can even play your own role in this vital part of the planet's well-being by giving your flowering plants a helping hand when it comes to pollination!

DID YOU KNOW...
When we talk about pollinators, we naturally think of bees, but pollination is helped along by a host of creatures including birds, bats and butterflies too!

> Plants pollinate by self-pollination or cross-pollination

WARNING
If you suffer from hay fever or asthma, it's vital that you don't overexpose yourself to pollen as it can bring on an asthma attack!

THE MAGIC OF POLLEN

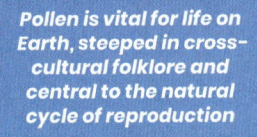

Pollen is vital for life on Earth, steeped in cross-cultural folklore and central to the natural cycle of reproduction

Wind in Pollination

Some plants are pollinated by pollen grains on the wind

Just as the wind scatters pollen, Navajo people scatter corn pollen as part of their rituals; symbolic of peace, light and prosperity, it is considered a gift fit for the gods. Navajo folklore even tells of the Pollen Path, which everyone takes through life.

Of course, anyone who has ever told the time or made a wish by blowing the seeds from a dandelion clock has been a part of a folklore ritual that goes back generations, whilst playing a vital role in wind-pollination too.

Water in Pollination

Water's role in pollination can be both positive and negative

Though rain can prevent pollination, it's vital for aquatic plants to spread the pollen that keeps the species reproducing. Indeed, a small amount of dew on the petals of a flower amplifies its fragrance, bringing pollinators flocking.

Next time you meditate around flowers, try focusing on the thought of a simple dew drop on a petal. Imagine the sun warming the dew and the fragrance in the air, summoning the pollinators who will carry the grains of pollen from plant to plant.

GREEN WITCHCRAFT

Help Pollination *happen*

1 Choose Direct Pollinating Flowers

Plants that pollinate directly don't need water, wind or pollinators to reproduce, so they're a great choice to get started.

2 Create a Haven for Pollinators

By choosing plants that appeal to pollinators, you can create a sanctuary where they will happily carry the pollen they collect from flower to flower.

3 Give the Pollinators a Drink

Make water available for pollinators to rest and refresh; use a shallow dish and add some pebbles, so smaller creatures have a safe place to drink.

Telling the Bees

The humble bee is vital to pollination and rich in folklore

To ancient Greeks and Romans, the bees were the messengers of the gods; this is just a small part of the cultural folklore around this most famous of all pollinators. They are central to the creation of the first human for Africa's Kalahari San people, fierce warriors in Native American mythology, and even the symbol of the hard-working people of industrial Manchester in the 19th century.

The custom of "telling the bees" is one that is believed to have begun in ancient Celtic lore, and involves the bees being informed when an important event has occurred in the household of their beekeeper, such as birth, marriage or death. In fact, when a beekeeper dies, their bees are placed in mourning by a member of the family. The person knocks politely on the hive and whispers or sings the sad news, allowing the bees to mourn their keeper and accept their new guardian.

THE MAGIC OF POLLEN

Bees play a vital role in pollination and have been steeped in folklore for centuries

❝ To ancient Greeks and Romans, the bees were the messengers of the gods

GREEN WITCHCRAFT

Bathe in Beauty

ROSES ARE A POTENT SYMBOL OF LOVE AND BEAUTY AND THE PERFECT INGREDIENT FOR A SELF-CARE SPELL TO ENHANCE YOUR POWERS OF ATTRACTION

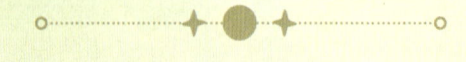

WORDS April Madden

Bathing has a long history in magical practise as a form of ritual cleansing and renewal

BATHE IN BEAUTY

Roses have been associated with love and beauty since ancient times. Sacred to the classical Greek goddess Aphrodite, they not only invoke her famous allure, but they're also packed with genuine cosmetic benefits, being soothing, anti-inflammatory and astringent. Their scent is refreshing and calming and one study even found that in some instances, women who smelled rose oil reported an easing of symptoms of depression and anxiety. This spell makes use of rose's physical and magical benefits to make you feel fabulous and is great preparation for a date, a night out, or whenever you want to look and feel your best.

If you have roses in your garden, picking two or three of them would be ideal. Otherwise, you can buy a small potted rose from a supermarket or garden store, or a simple small bouquet. Red or pink roses are best, but any will do. You'll also need rosewater – you can find this at a good value price in a supermarket baking aisle – rose essential oil, bath salts made from Himalayan pink salt, a rose scented candle (or a plain pink candle anointed with rose essential oil), and a rose-based moisturiser, facial oil or face mask of your choice.

Aphrodite, the ancient Greek goddess of love and beauty, is often associated with the rose

> **One study found that women who smelled rose oil reported an easing of symptoms of depression and anxiety**

Rose essential oil has a wide range of uses in both cosmetics and magic, and is a useful addition to any green witch's store cupboard

Put the bouquet of roses in your bathroom, light the candle, and run a bath with a handful of the pink Himalayan salts, a generous splash of rosewater and a few drops of rose essential oil. While the bath is running, cleanse your face and apply the rose moisturiser, facial oil or mask. Once the bath is run, step in and scatter some rose petals on the water's surface. Breathe deeply and inhale the scent of roses all around you. If you wish, you can invoke Aphrodite and ask her to bless you with her gifts of attraction. Otherwise, simply visualise your bath soaked in golden-pink rosy light and feel yourself relax and absorb its beautifying power.

When you're finished, dry off and follow your regular after-bath skincare routine. You could even add rose body lotion or perfume if you choose.

You'll Need...

- A small bouquet of roses (from your garden if possible, otherwise shop-bought)
- Rose petals (from one of the roses)
- Rose water
- A rose scented candle, or a pink candle
- Rose essential oil
- Himalayan pink bath salts
- Rose facial oil, face mask or moisturiser

ALTERNATIVELY

If you don't have or can't use a bathtub, substitute the Himalayan pink salts with a rose scented shower gel, oil or soap in the shower instead

GREEN WITCHCRAFT

Plant Power

PLANTS PROVIDE AN EASY WAY TO CONNECT WITH NATURE AND THE EARTH ELEMENT

WORDS Peg Aloi

WHY NOT TRY...

Immersing yourself in nature can be done in very simple ways. Finding a favourite park bench to sit on, installing a bird feeder in your yard to attract songbirds, or just taking a walk in your town and finding points of natural beauty you have never noticed before

Growth & Fertility

Plant seeds to manifest growth, abundance or fertility

Planting is a powerful activity: we plant seeds expecting them to grow into something useful, beautiful or nourishing. The symbolic action of planting seeds can also be used for magical purposes. Planting seeds can represent something we wish to grow in our lives, such as a business, or an intentional community. Seeds are also a symbol of fertility. Planting seeds in an intentional way is also a way to conjure abundance: this might include having a healthier financial situation or making friends after moving to a new place. Plant your seeds in a pot or in the ground while speaking aloud the magical purpose of your spell. Repeat this every day when watering the seeds and continue to visualise your goals. As the seeds begin to sprout and grow, focus on how the aspects of abundance, fertility or growth are being called forth to be manifested in your life.

PLANT POWER

For your seed magic, choose a flower, vegetable or herb that is special to you, or connected to your goal and intention

Moon Phase Planting

Gardening with moon phases helps ou attune to the moon cycle

Using the phases of the moon for gardening is a well-known traditional practice. This method observes moon phases for the timing of certain tasks: planting when the moon is waxing, and pruning or weeding when the moon is waning. The moon also moves through the zodiac signs. The signs are all considered either "fruitful" or "barren" to varying degrees. Find out more about gardening with the moon on p86.

> The symbolic action of planting seeds can also be used for magic

Benefits of Houseplants

Houseplants are pleasing to look at and provide many physical and mental health benefits

Houseplants can enhance living spaces in many ways. Plants produce oxygen via photosynthesis and help purify the air. The organic shapes and textures of houseplants can be utilised to balance feng shui elements in your home. Some plants have pleasant fragrances. The colour green is associated with calming, healing, and harmony. Plants provide a natural antidote to our technology-driven lives. Caring for plants indoors help us feel connected to nature all year round.

WHY NOT TRY...

Even if you don't have space to garden, growing a pot of herbs on your balcony or in a sunny window can be a fulfilling activity that gives you fresh fragrant herbs for cooking, tea or an uplifting source of natural fragrance. Most herbs grow very easily from seed

Image Getty Images

47

GREEN WITCHCRAFT

Victorian Flower Language

The Victorians developed a complex lexicon of symbolic meaning associated with flowers that has implications for esoteric and magical work

In the Victorian era, many areas of study became the source of social trends, including aspects of nature. Floriography was a system of meaning assigned to various flowers and other plants that allowed for a silent, symbolic "language" to be communicated between a giver and recipient. This language was connected to the flowers themselves, guiding the choices of what to include in a bouquet, and also in the way they were presented or received (using the right or left hand denoted different meanings, for example). This "secret language" was understood to be a rather thrilling way to communicate, as it allowed for passionate feelings (like romantic love) to be conveyed within the confines of strict social etiquette. The meanings assigned to various flowers have survived to this day and there's been revived interest in this tradition recently. The public took notice of the flowers chosen by Kate Middleton for her wedding bouquet (like myrtle and ivy, signifying love and marriage), and the plants King Charles III chose for his mother's funeral wreath, including rosemary, associated with remembrance. Choosing flowers for spellcraft can be a mindful act of preparation and intention. Flowers can be placed on your altar, made into a charm or garland, or added to incense. You can adapt outdated Victorian meanings for your purposes. For example, the Victorians associated daisies with purity and innocence; for you, they might symbolise a new beginning.

The Wood Wide Web

Scientists have discovered a vast network of growth that can connect trees and plants

In 1997 researcher Suzanne Simard made an extraordinary hypothesis about the natural world. It took until 2015 when an ecologist named Thomas Crowther gathered data about trees and their connection to fungus, bacteria and other growing things for her revelatory research to be accepted. While scientist James Lovelock formulated the "Gaia Hypothesis" in the 1970s, based on the idea that the Earth was a system of interlocking living systems that formed one large consciousness (named for the Greek earth goddess), Simard's theory, dubbed the "wood wide web," explicitly shows that trees are linked by vast networks of underground growth. The idea that every living thing on Earth is connected in this way has profound implications for humanity. The choices we make as individuals can directly impact all the Earth's living things, and this knowledge can make us more mindful of our role as human stewards and caretakers of our planet.

Benefits of Herbs

Herbs have many culinary and medicinal benefits and are easy to grow

Herbs can be enjoyed in many ways: fresh herbs may be added to salads, soups, or other dishes. Dried herbs can also be used for cooking or made into a tea or infusion. The volatile essential oils in herbs give them their vibrant flavours and aromas which provide a range of physical and mental health benefits. Hot herbal tea is an excellent soothing, warming drink in cold weather, or can be chilled with ice in summer.

PLANT POWER

Edible Gardens

Few things are as satisfying as growing your own food

It's been said that contemporary culture is disconnected from nature, and this is very apparent in our relationship to food. We buy food ready-made in boxes and bags, but do we understand where it comes from? Growing our own food can have a profound impact on our mental and physical wellbeing. Growing fruits, vegetables or herbs can enhance our connection to nature and promote a mindful approach to nourishing ourselves.

Forest Bathing

Immersing yourself in nature can provide a boost to your mental and physical wellbeing

Forest bathing is a concept invented in Japan in the 1980s, where "shinrin-yoku" refers to visiting a forest setting for relaxation and rejuvenation. At the time, the idea was not just to foster wellbeing by connecting to nature and taking a break from modern technology, but also to raise awareness of the ecological vulnerability of Japan's forests, and to encourage their protection. The practice became popular, and scientific studies showed that spending time in nature provided many physical and mental health benefits. The idea is to fully embrace being in nature, with all its sights, sounds and sensations, and not use smartphones or other distracting devices during that time. One need not to go an actual forest to practice forest bathing. Any natural green place, such as a park or a garden, can provide a rejuvenating retreat for those who seek nature's healing energy, and help to soothe mind, body and spirit.

Cultivating your own flowers, herbs or edible plants can be both a mindful and magical exercise

Images Getty Images

GREEN WITCHCRAFT

Druid *tree* Wisdom

SACRED TREES ARE COMMON IN MANY CULTURES, BUT FOR THE CELTS THEY WERE HOME TO REVERED NATURE SPIRITS AND PROTECTIVE GUARDIANS THAT STOOD LIKE NATURAL MOMENTS, AT WHICH THEY HELD THEIR RELIGIOUS CEREMONIES

WORDS Alice Pattillo

DID YOU KNOW…
Trees symbolise life, rebirth and protection and are seen as portals to other realms – whether it's the land of the gods or home to the fae

Trees have been held sacred in Western culture since at least the Iron Age. Trees were often seen as links between the mortal and supernatural realms, their roots and branches reaching into other worlds, as well as protective entities thanks to their strong wood (an important commodity) and extensive lifespans.

The druids held trees in particular reverence – the word druid is thought to have derived from a Celtic word meaning "knower of the oak", their most sacred tree. These ancient priests and sorcerers led Celtic religion. Their churches were groves, and trees were seen as wise spirits – the Irish believed that the trees were home to the spirits of their ancestors. While the druids died out, their influence continued through folklore customs and modern druidry, which grew out of the 19th century Celtic Revival movement. Many British surnames are derived from the names of trees that each family perhaps once worked with, associated themselves with and held sacred or within which their familiar spirit was linked. Place names also often reference trees, demonstrating their importance to the area.

Sacred Species

Celtic mythology tells of the five Guardian Trees of Ireland, kings of all trees and protectors of the provinces. Each is one of the three species the druids held most sacred (oak, ash and yew) and has a name: Eó Mugna (oak), Bile Tortan (ash), Eó Ruis (yew), Craeb Daithí (ash) and Craeb Uisnig (ash).

Oak
Represents strength, wisdom, healing, success, protection and are often credited as the Celtic tree of life. Druids performed sacrificial and ritualistic rites in oak groves. In modern Pagan lore, the Oak King rules the summer half of the year.

Ash
The Norse world tree, the Yggdrasil, which connects all nine worlds of the gods, supernatural and mortals. A protective tree believed to protect against evil spirits as well as having healing medicinal properties.

Yew
A symbol of resilience. Perhaps the only evergreen tree in Britain at one time. Its 'eternal life' links it to death, rebirth, reincarnation and resurrection. Staves of yew were reputedly used for carving Ogham letters used for magic.

DRUID TREE WISDOM

Both ancient and modern druids venerate the power of trees, with worship being practised out of doors at stone circles or in sacred groves

Woodland Words

The Celts developed their own runic alphabet, the Beith-luis-nin, also referred to as the Ogham alphabet, which could easily be formed with twigs for divination or scratched into surfaces to leave messages, and can be found carved into stones in Ireland and Wales. Each of its 20 letters is ascribed a different meaning (in a similar fashion to the Nordic runes) which medieval scholars deciphered as mostly trees or shrubs, earning it the name the Celtic Tree Alphabet. They are as follows:

A	- Ailm (Fir)		O	- Onn (Ash)
B	- Beithe (Birch)		Q	- Quert/Cert (Apple)
C	- Coll (Hazel)		R	- Ruis (Elder)
D	- Duit/Dair (Oak)		S	- Sail (Willow)
E	- Eadhadh/Edad (Aspen)		T	- Tinne (Holly)
F/W	- Fearn (Alder)		U	- Úr (Heather)
G	- Gort (Ivy)		Z	- Straif (Blackthorn)
H/J	- Uath (Hawthorn)			
I	- Idad/Iodhadh (Yew)			
L	- Luis (Rowan)			
M	- Muin (Vine)			
N	- Nion/Nin (Ash)			

When used in divination, the Ogham alphabet can be interpreted using the meanings and associations ascribed to each tree in Celtic lore.

GREEN WITCHCRAFT

Embrace the Path of the Hedgewitch

INSPIRED BY HISTORICAL CUNNING FOLK, THE BORDERLINES BETWEEN SOCIETY AND THE WILDERNESS ARE A HEDGEWITCH'S DOMAIN

WORDS Alice Pattillo

Do you enjoy foraging in forests and feel a strong connection to nature? Mixing herbal remedies and blending teas? Prefer the company of animals to socialising with people? The solitary pagan pathway of hedgewitchery could be your calling.

Hedgewitchery is a form of traditional witchcraft inspired by the cunning folk of old. The term, used most often in the United Kingdom, conjures up images of the wise woman or midwife who lived on the fringes of the forest in a remote cottage shrouded by hedgerows at the edge of town, outside of mainstream society. These local herbalist healers were experts of nature, offering locals basic medical care, herbal potions, advice and ancient wisdom. They were also subject to persecution and derision, and it's often said that they were the first to be branded a witch and blamed for societal ills during the era of the witch trials as their knowledge posed a threat to the church.

The path of a hedgewitch is, therefore, a solitary one, deeply rooted in nature, healing and traditional folk wisdom. There is no wrong or right way to practise hedgewitchery – just as long as you are honouring and guided by Mother Nature. Whether you are drawn to the mountains, forests, plants and herbalism, the rivers and streams, or animals and traditional rural lore, they all have a place in hedgewitchery.

Eating Green

Many hedgewitches stick to an organic and natural diet informed by seasonal produce. While it's not a requirement to eat a vegan or vegetarian diet as a hedgewitch, many do follow a plant-based diet – but it is entirely up to you and your personal dietary requirements. Whatever you choose, it is important to be mindful of your food and be in harmony with nature, so an ethical diet – even if this includes some responsibly sourced meat – is essential. Try visiting local farmers' markets and foraging for food yourself. If you've got a green thumb, you might even want to start growing your own produce!

HEDGEWITCHERY

WHY NOT TRY...

Embrace the old ways and look into the folk traditions and lore of your local area. What customs inspire you? Which deities and myths resonate with you? Incorporate them into your practise

Hedgewitchcraft is inspired by the idea of solitary practitioners following their own green path of magical practise close to nature

Images Getty Images

53

GREEN WITCHCRAFT

> **Living the path of a green or hedgewitch is an organic process**

Hedgewitches are solitary creatures who prefer the solace of the woods, animals and traditions

Living the Path

Unlike other pagan pathways, there are no hard and fast rules for a hedgewitch

Other modern witchcraft religions, such as Wicca, include joining an established coven and abiding by a set belief structure and practices. High magic – often called ceremonial, learned or ritual magic – includes undergoing initiation, subscribing to a series of occult teachings and strictly orchestrated ceremonies within a magical organisation – often an elite, secret society – and is kept separate from everyday life. This is a direct contrast to hedgewitchery, which is essentially a way of life. This unstructured form of natural folk magic is learned through trial and error, and has no hierarchy or structure or even any need to collaborate with anyone else. Living the path of a green or hedgewitch is an organic process, relaxed and individual to every practitioner, with each witch in charge of their own pathway, beliefs and constructing their own unique grimoire, simply using nature, intuition and inherited wisdom as their guide.

HEDGEWITCHERY

How to be a Hedgewitch

Letting the earth guide you

You can learn hedgewitchcraft from nature itself: embracing the sunlight, harnessing the energies of the moon, watching wildlife and observing the seasons. You may wish to delve further into books, research native traditions, folk customs and countryside lore, the properties of plants and trees or herbal magic and hone your craft through practice. Some hedgewitches devote themselves to old nature-based deities such as the fae or nymphs or connecting with forest-dwelling creatures, while others focus on the changing of the seasons and traditional festivals. Hedgewitchcraft is a way of life, a life in which you let nature and its nurturing, healing energies guide you. In terms of spellwork, many perform small, everyday rituals such as brewing tea, blending herbal remedies or incense, sweeping to cleanse their space or foraging for food and connecting with the earth and spirit realm through meditation. Trances and divination work using all that nature has to offer – flowers and herbs, the sun and moon, crystals and animals.

Try a Seasonal Sweep Routine

1 Grab your broom

Take a natural fibre broomstick at the time of each new moon, or the new moon nearest to each solstice and equinox. This ritual is particularly potent during the Spring Equinox!

2 Centre yourself at the heart of your home

Stand in the middle of your room, holding your broom, and focus on your intention – to sweep stale energy and negativity, purify, protect and attract prosperity for the season ahead.

3 Clear the cobwebs!

Begin sweeping right to left in a quick motion, moving counterclockwise to banish negative energy. Ensure you sweep all corners of your home, window sills and door frames and, of course, end at the door to cast out and banish. Visualise the negativity leaving your home and a new, bright light of fresh energy and prosperity entering its place.

GREEN WITCHCRAFT

Divine Inspiration

MANY GREEN WITCHES FEEL AN INFINITY TO ANCIENT ANIMISTIC BELIEF SYSTEMS INFORMED BY NATURE DEITIES AND FOLKLORIC SUPERNATURAL BEINGS

WORDS Alice Pattillo

Both structured and unstructured modern Pagan pathways stray away from the belief in one omniscient god common to many mainstream religions, and instead look back to ancient polytheistic pantheons, animism and folklore to inform their craft.

Before the rise of monotheistic Abrahamic religions (Judaism, Christianity and Islam), most people believed in animism or polytheism (often an extension of animistic beliefs). Animism is the belief that everything possesses a spirit and is the earliest form of religion. Animism includes nature worship and, more often than not, the belief in multiple gods and goddesses (polytheism), including nature-based deities or personifications of nature, natural phenomena and other supernatural creatures heavily associated with aspects of the natural world. Aspects of animism can be seen as the basis of many ancient polytheistic belief systems and folk religions throughout the world, including the Egyptian gods, the Greek and Roman pantheons, the Norse Æsir and Vanir and the Aztec gods, as well as Buddhism, Hinduism and Sikhism. Mythical stories, folklore and traditions have kept these beliefs alive after the expansion of the Religions of the Book, along with some Indigenous tribes and nations who have continued to practise their traditions for centuries without conversion to Abrahamic religions.

As a result, there are numerous deities and pantheons that a green witch may choose to devote themselves to, it just depends on which you feel resonate with you most.

DEITIES

DID YOU KNOW…
The portals to the land of the fae are often located within Stone Age monuments, caves, hawthorn trees, wells and upon hills – why not go for a walk and try to find one?

The fae are fond of dancing, particularly within their "fairy circles" formed of mushrooms

The Way of the Fae

These mythical creatures are found in the folklore across Europe

Also known as fair folk or faeries, the fae are often seen as ancient deities in pagan belief systems, as spirits of nature, or a magical, hidden race of people. They are also often linked to the dead and their realm to the afterlife. Members of the fair folk include goblins, brownies, sprites, elves and gnomes. They are believed to have magical powers and are often perceived as nature's protectors, residing in an unseen realm located beneath the earth. Particularly prevalent in Celtic and British folklore, they are named the Sìthe in Scotland and are divided into the Seelie (benevolent tricksters) and the Unseelie (the malevolent fae). In Ireland, they are the Aos Sí ("people of the fairy mounds") and in Wales they are dubbed the Tylwyth Teg ("fair family").

The fae are peaceful folk but often mischievous and malicious when offended. They enjoy dancing and making fairy rings made of mushrooms and hold rowan trees sacred. In the form of will-o'-the-wisps, the fae have been known to both aid and lead lone travellers astray, depending on how they were treated. There are numerous tales of humans being kidnapped or lured into the realm of the fae, particularly when the veil between worlds was thinnest – at Samhain. During this time, people took measures to repel and appease the fae. Offerings of baked goods, particularly bread, were said to keep you in their good books. Iron would keep trickster fae at bay while protection could be found in the form of charms made from either the herb St John's Wort or four-leaf clovers.

> ❝ Animism is the belief that everything possesses a spirit and is the earliest form of religion

GREEN WITCHCRAFT

Meet *your* Familiar

1 Enter a meditative state

Begin your search by finding a quiet space and sitting comfortably. Close your eyes and envision a white light surrounding you, drawing you into the clearing of a woodland or natural setting.

2 Let your guide come to you

Imagine yourself in your preferred natural setting and invoke the presence of your familiar. Repeat out loud, "I call upon you, my familiar, manifested from Mother Nature. Reveal yourself to me, my friend, my spirit guide, be here with me now", or something similar.

3 Say hello to your familiar spirit

You should see a vision of an animal – it may be a bird, a small mammal, a reptile or an amphibian. Demand to see their true nature. If it glows gold, silver, white or rainbow, it is your familiar – welcome and bond with it. If it doesn't glow one these colours, banish it into a cloud of golden light and try again.

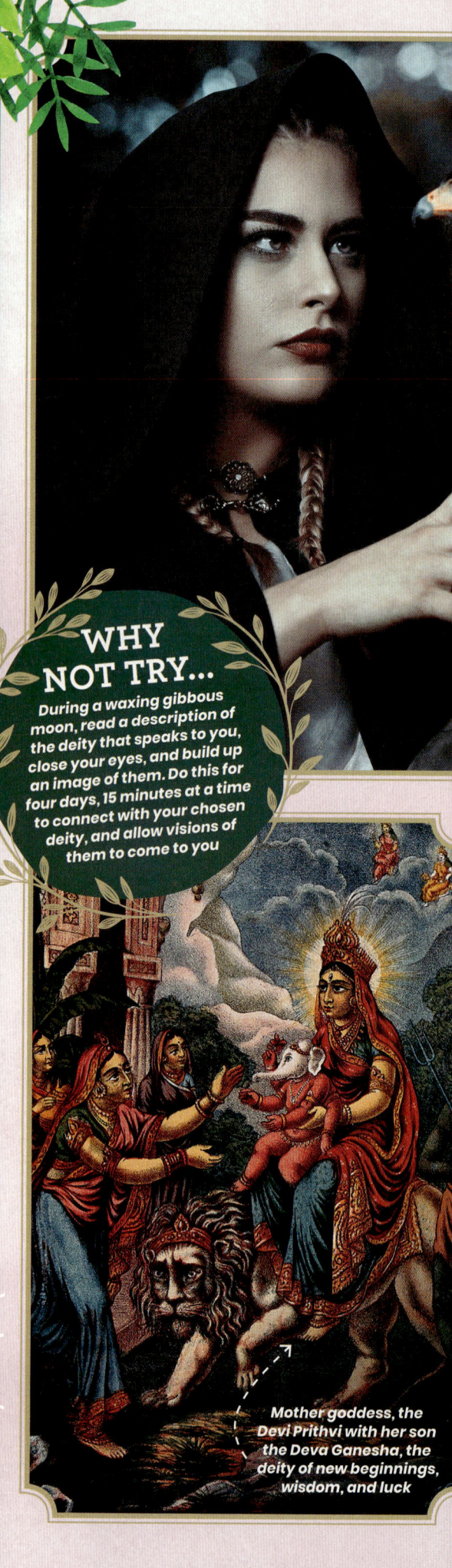

WHY NOT TRY…
During a waxing gibbous moon, read a description of the deity that speaks to you, close your eyes, and build up an image of them. Do this for four days, 15 minutes at a time to connect with your chosen deity, and allow visions of them to come to you

Mother goddess, the Devi Prithvi with her son the Deva Ganesha, the deity of new beginnings, wisdom, and luck

DEITIES

Popular forms familiars would take include cats, dogs, owls, frogs, toads, rats, birds, ferrets and hares

Familiars

The witch's cat is a familiar trope, but these guardians are much more than pets

Familiars are supernatural entities that protect, serve and assist witches in their magical practice. In the medieval and early modern periods, they were considered either malevolent demons or benevolent fairies, depending on whom they were assisting. Familiar spirits most often manifest as an animal but are also able to appear as a human or humanoid figure. Witches would meet their familiar in a variety of ways. Often, it would simply appear to her spontaneously, particularly during times of hardship (like that stray cat who wandered into your home when you were having a bad day and never left!) but it could also have been inherited from a family member or conjured through a spell. In some cases, the witch would then enter into a formal agreement or make a pact with the familiar, but in others it was simply an unspoken, mutual understanding.

Familiars may be perceived to be the witch's alter ego or type of spirit guide with a psychic connection to the witch, who connects her to another realm – or, according to witch hunters, the devil. Traditionally, witches and cunning folk fed their familiars with anything from blood and meat to milk and bread.

Nature Spirits

Devas, Dryads and other divine beings personify and protect every aspect of the natural world

In nature worshipping religions, there are deities in charge of most forces of nature. From earth, water and vegetation to fire, sky, sun and air, a supernatural being oversees every aspect of our world and beyond.

The Sanskrit word for divine being is deva. The Vedas – ancient Indian texts that inform both Hinduism and Buddhism – tell us of the benevolent Devas and malevolent Asuras. The Devas are male personifications and deities, each representing a force of nature or moral value. These include the creation god Brahma, as well as Shiva and Vishnu, while the force of nature deities are considered lesser Devas and include Vayu (wind), Varuna (water) and Agni (fire). The Vedas also mention Devis (goddesses) which include Prithvi (earth) and Aranyani (forest), and lesser nature spirits called Yakshas (male) and Yakshini (female). This concept has been adopted by the New Age movement, where "deva" is used as a generic term to describe any spiritual force or being behind nature, including other nature spirits such as fairies and ancient Greek nymphs. Nymphs are female lesser deities and personifications of nature or nature spirits. They are split into subgroups that include Dryads (oak tree nymphs), Meliae (ash tree nymphs), Epimelides (fruit tree nymphs), Daphnaie (laurel tree nymphs) Nereids (sea nymphs, which included the Oceanids, whose brothers were the Potamai river gods), Naiads (freshwater nymphs, daughters of the Potamai) and Oreads (mountain nymphs). In Santeria and the Yoruba religions of West Africa, nature spirits are known as Orisha and are sent by the creator god, Olodumare, to assist humanity and teach them.

> **In nature worshipping religions, there are deities in charge of most forces of nature**

GREEN WITCHCRAFT

Deities

GAIA
Ancient Greek

The Mother Nature earth goddess archetype is found all across the globe as an important creator deity, from Roman Terra to the Incan Pachamama, but the primordial Greek goddess Gaia is perhaps the most famous. A personification of the earth itself – from which all other gods and goddesses are spawned, including Uranus (the Sky) and Oceanus (the Sea) – before Gaia there was only chaos. She is associated with life itself, the snake, the colours green and brown, and bay leaves.

RA
Ancient Egyptian

Ra was one of the most important deities in Ancient Egypt. He was a falcon-headed (and occasionally ram-headed) sun god who ruled all of the created world including the sky, earth and underworld, earning him the title "master of all life" and inspiring the Egyptians to build the pyramids in his honor. From Ra came Nut (goddess of the sky), Geb (earth god), Shu (the god of air, wind and lions) and Tefnut (the goddess of rain, dew and moist air) among others.

CERNUNNOS
Celtic

This horned god is often called Lord of the Animals or Lord of the Wild Things and is depicted seated, like a shaman, with antler horns and surrounded by animals such as stags, ram-horned serpents, dogs, rats and bulls. He often holds a bag of coins or grains and wears a torc (linking him to wealth, luck and power) and is said to be a peaceful deity of nature and fruitfulness.

ENKI (EA)
Mesopotamian

The god of water, particularly life-giving fresh water such as springs, rivers and lakes, Enki is also associated with earth and creation, wisdom and magic. He is a co-creator of life and the world and therefore a fertility god, often dubbed the Lord of Semen. His symbols are the goat and the fish.

Oshun
Yoruban

The goddess Oshun is an important river deity in Ifá oral tradition, Yoruba-based religions of West Africa, Haitian Voodoo and Santeria. She represents femininity, purity, fertility, romantic love and beauty. She is associated with fresh water sources such as waterfalls, streams, canals and, of course, rivers, and she is associated with the colours white, yellow and gold. In Brazil she is also called "Lady of Gold".

DEITIES

MEDEINA
Lithuanian

In numerous religions, the forest is seen as a female entity, or it is at least guarded by female spirits. The Hindu forest devi is Aranyani, while in Yoruba belief the forest orisha is Ajá. In Lithuania, the forest is overseen by Medeina (literally meaning forest or tree) who is one of the most important deities in Lithuanian mythology. She rules and protects the forests, trees and animals, holds hares sacred and is associated with wolves. She is also a huntress goddess, similar to the Roman Diana and the Greek Artemis and Slavic Devana.

Pan
Greek

The god of the wild was a significant Renaissance figure and remains important to the Neopagan movement. His companions include the nymphs and he appears as a faun or satyr – with the hindlegs and horns of a goat. He rules over fields, groves, woodlands and shepherds and is associated with sex, fertility and the spring. His Roman counterpart is Faunus.

MORANA
Slavic

The goddess of vegetation, death and winter, Morana is the Slavic equivalent of the Irish Caillech. Burning or drawing an effigy of Morana (also known as Marzanna) at the end of winter is a custom that continues in Poland, Czechia, Lithuania and Slovakia. After this ritual, the spring goddess Kostroma returns (like Brigid in Irish myth). She is often also associated with the Slavic equivalent of Diana or Artemis, Devana, who is the goddess of forests, wildlife, the moon and hunting, and associated with mares, bears and wolves.

SKADI
Norse

Pictured on skis hunting the vast mountains of Scandinavia, Skadi is a giantess and the Norse goddess of the wilderness. She is associated with ice, winter, the mountains, skiing and bowhunting. Beautiful and a formidable warrior, Skadi earned her place in Asgard by demanding to marry a god. Her sacred animals include the wolf, snow leopards and bears and she symbolises endurance, strength, survival and courage. She is stormy and unpredictable but full of passion – relentless in her pursuit of justice.

HECATE
Greek

Hecate is a moon deity associated with herbs and poisonous plants, witchcraft, crossroads, boundaries and protection, death and the underworld, travel and night-time. Her domains stretch across the sky (heavens), earth and sea (or underworld) making her a "Trivia" (three-way) goddess whereby she holds three distinct aspects, leading to her functioning as the crone aspect of the Wiccan triple goddess. She is associated with dogs and snakes and her symbols include a key or a pair of torches.

> **The Mother Nature earth goddess archetype is found all across the globe**

GREEN WITCHCRAFT

The Wheel of the Year

THE WHEEL OF THE YEAR, MARKING THE CYCLICAL PROGRESSION OF THE SEASONS, IS AN IMPORTANT FEATURE IN THE LIVES OF MANY PAGANS TODAY

WORDS Willow Winsham

The idea of the year as a wheel, cycling through the four seasons in a never-ending journey from darkness to light, features with varying degrees of prominence in the beliefs of many modern Pagans. Although there are variations between groups and locations, the Wheel of the Year generally marks eight (or in some cases four) seasonal festivals that celebrate the cyclic nature of the world around us.

Linked to the annual journey of the Sun and the birth, death, and rebirth of the gods, the wheel is based on the natural solar divisions of the solstices and equinoxes, with four of the festivals – Ostara, Litha, Mabon and Yule – marking these quarter days of the year. The two solstices mark the point when the Sun reaches its highest point in the sky at each pole, and thus the longest and shortest days of the year, the start of summer and winter. By contrast, as the name implies, the two equinoxes are the points when the sun is directly above the equator, with day and night being of almost equal length and heralding the start of spring and autumn. Imbolc, Beltane, Lughnasadh and Samhain, the remaining four festivals, mark a seasonal midpoint between each, and are known as cross quarter days. Although attempts have been made to prove a direct continuity from the past to the present, historically, evidence suggests that in practice, the wheel of eight festivals was not celebrated in its current form until recent times. There were many variations in what was celebrated and when, and the cycle that is now observed was not in place for our ancestors. For instance, Celtic practice may have focused on the cross quarter days, while Anglo Saxons observed the quarter days for their celebrations. Under the influence of Robert Graves, Gerald Gardner and others, by the mid 20th century, the Wheel of the Year and the festivals within it, were familiar terminology within Pagan communities. The ways in which the festivals are celebrated today however does have roots in folklore practices and traditions. The focus now as then were community sabbats or celebrations, coming together to give thanks, with offerings made to nature, the deities or spirits revered on a collective or individual level.

> "By the mid 20th century, the Wheel of the Year and the festivals within it, were familiar terminology"

THE WHEEL OF THE YEAR

DID YOU KNOW...
The most common names and those most familiar today for the celebrations marked by the wheel are of Germanic or Celtic origin

63

GREEN WITCHCRAFT

Yule

THE WHEEL OF THE YEAR, MARKING THE CYCLICAL PROGRESSION OF THE SEASONS, IS AN IMPORTANT FEATURE IN THE LIVES OF MANY PAGANS TODAY

WORDS Willow Winsham

The midwinter festival celebrated on 21 December is most commonly known today as Yule. Of pre-Christian origin, with connections that span back to the Neolithic period and perhaps beyond, Yule takes place at the midwinter solstice, or the longest night, the day when, in the northern hemisphere, the north pole is tilted furthest away from the Sun.

A time of hope and rebirth, Yule brings with it the promise of gradually lengthening days and the return of the Sun and the warmth it brings. The focus of the celebrations is the idea of light coming forth out of darkness, along with the death of the Sun and subsequent rebirth. The Holly King who rules over the dark half of the year is believed by many to give way to the Oak King, who brings with him the returning light.

Yule has connections with other midwinter festivals such as Saturnalia, the ancient Roman festival celebrated between 17 and 23 December. This precursor of many future midwinter celebrations was held in the name of Saturn, and was a time of great feasting and merriment. Saturnalia is best known as a festival of social subversion, when slaves could speak their mind without repercussions, and were feasted by their masters. It also shares obvious similarities with Christmas, with much of the same imagery and traditions adopted by the later Christian festival.

One of the most popular traditions is the Yule log. Amidst much revelry, the selected branch was taken into the house and set in the hearth, decorated, then doused with spirits. Using a section from the previous Yule log, kept for that purpose, the new log was lit, with the idea that celebrations continue as long as it burns. Nothing was wasted, with the ashes used to protect fields and enhance the fertility of the soil.

The use of greenery is also prominent, with evergreens used for decoration and symbolism throughout. Holly, pine, ivy and oak are common, often on windowsills or doorways or fashioned into wreaths. These are seen as signs of life everlasting, immortality, protection, healing, regeneration and rebirth. Mistletoe is also closely associated with Yule, both as protection from evil and as a sign of fertility. The familiar colours associated with Yule, red, green and white, reflect the significance of these plants and trees. Beware though, they must be removed by Twelfth Night, in order to avoid bad luck for the year to come.

DID YOU KNOW...
Many midwinter festivals have similar themes, such as the birth or return of a god, symbolically linked to the sun

YULE

Mistletoe is associated with Yule. In Roman tradition it symbolises protection while travelling through the underworld, as in the Aeneid

> ❝ The focus of the celebrations is light coming forth out of darkness

This Holly King figure stands in South Barrule in the UK's Isle of Man. He represents the energy of the dark half of the year, between midsummer and the winter festival Yule

With its distinctive red berries and sharp leaves, at Yule holly represents the shift from the dark half of the year into the light

Images Alamy, Getty Images

65

GREEN WITCHCRAFT

Imbolc

THE STIRRINGS OF SPRING, MARKING THE END OF THE DARK HALF OF THE YEAR, IMBOLC WAS CELEBRATED WITH CANDLES, RUSHES, AND THE PRESENCE OF THE GODDESS BRIGID

WORDS Willow Winsham

DID YOU KNOW...
Imbolc is sometimes referred to as Candlemas, after the Christian festival of motherhood and light held around the same time

The festival of Imbolc was, historically, another of the four seasonal celebrations observed by Gaelic communities during the year. Taking place on 1 February, this festival marked the start of spring, with all the hope, wonder and enthusiasm that time heralded.

Unlike some celebrations of more recent origin, Imbolc appears to have held an important place in the Irish calendar from at least the 10th century. Like many such traditions, the exact origin of the name is uncertain. Suggestions include derivation from the old Irish word for cleansing, or, another suggestion, the meaning "in the belly" as a nod to the ewes that were expectant at that time of year.

Brigid, originally as a pagan goddess and then as a Christian saint, is an important Imbolc figure. Although practices varied, the idea that Brigid ushered in the lighter days of spring, leading people from the dark half of the year, was central to her part in Imbolc traditions. Deeply venerated, she was invited into households as an honoured guest, where she was variously feasted, entertained and invited to sleep in a specially prepared bed. Households would leave small objects in the hope Brigid would bless them when she visited on Imbolc eve. Rushes or reeds also played a big part; in Northern Ireland they were carried as a symbolic Brigid circled the household, some were laid out on the floor, fashioned into crosses, or used to make the saint a bed to sleep in.

Brideogs, representations of Brigid made from reeds and dressed in cloth and flowers, were familiar sights in both Ireland and Scotland. Processions took them from house to house, where gifts and further decoration were bestowed upon them, before the figure was feasted and laid to rest for the night.

The purifying nature of fire was significant, with candles marking a reminder of the promise of the Sun returning as the year unfolded. Today, Brigid is at the heart of Pagan Imbolc celebrations. Imbolc also has links to the Gaelic winter hag, the Cailleach. As tradition goes, it is at Imbolc that she collects wood for her fire to see her through to the end of the winter. A sunny Imbolc enabled her to collect more, and thus foretold a long winter. If the weather at Imbolc is bad, then winter will soon be over, as the Cailleach would not have enough firewood to last. Today, Imbolc is celebrated in a variety of forms.

In a recent Imbolc celebration, the Green Man and Jack Frost do battle for control of the seasons: spring emerges triumphant

IMBOLC

Fire and candles are an important part of Imbolc celebrations, symbolising the light of the returning spring sun

Flowers such as the snowdrop are among the first to signal the changing of the seasons, as Imbolc ushers in the spring

"The purifying nature of fire was significant"

Images Getty Images

67

GREEN WITCHCRAFT

Ostara

MODERN CELEBRATION, WORSHIP OF AN ANCIENT GODDESS, OR THE ORIGIN OF EASTER; WHAT DO EGGS, HARES AND CHURCH FATHERS HAVE TO DO WITH THE SPRING EQUINOX?

WORDS Willow Winsham

Ostara is a festival of spring time. Usually celebrated by many at the time of the spring equinox, falling between 19 and 22 March each year, the overarching theme of this celebration, observed by many Pagans today, is that of new beginnings, new life, fertility and renewal. One of the times of year when the nights and days are of equal length, Ostara heralds the shift towards longer, lighter days, the beginning of new cycles of life amidst nature, and the celebration of the Spring Maiden, with her promise of fertility and renewal. Flowers, eggs and rabbits are all strongly associated with modern Ostara and its celebrations.

Ostara, or Eostre is believed by many to be the goddess of this festival, and holds significance for many modern Pagans in their celebrations at this time of year. Ideas about the goddess include origins as an ancient goddess of the dawn, or a fertility goddess, though her biggest association is with the bringing of spring.

But what were the origins of this popular goddess? The only historical reference to Eostre comes from the writings of church father, Bede. He refers to the old name for April, Eosturmonata, and his assumption it marked the celebration of a Germanic goddess of that name. The writings of 19th century folklorist Jacob Grimm helped further perpetuate and popularise the idea. His was the first mention of the Germanic Ostara, and it is from his work that most 'ancient facts' regarding the goddess actually stem from. Other fallacies frequently repeated regarding Ostara and Eostre include an assumed etymological link to the word oestrogen, and links with the Assyrian goddess Ishtar. Hares, eggs and bunnies were also absent from the historical festival until amalgamated into it by Jacob Grimm, but have, thanks to the promulgation of his work, become associated with modern celebrations of Ostara.

Although debate exists today over whether Bede outright invented Eostre for purposes that remain unclear, this does little to diminish her popularity. A tale with origins in the 19th century tells of how the goddess was late to bring the spring one year. As a result, a small bird died, much to the grief of a little girl who found it. What did the goddess do? She turned the poor creature into a snow hare, the magical creature delighting the child by laying rainbow coloured eggs. Each year, the goddess told the girl, watch for the arrival of the snow hare. For then everyone would know that spring had arrived.

Hundreds gather at Stonehenge each year to watch the sun rise that marks the dawn of the spring equinox

OSTARA

DID YOU KNOW...
Many of the modern associations between Ostara and Easter traditions stem from the 19th century writings of Jacob Grimm on the topic

GREEN WITCHCRAFT

Beltane

AMIDST FIRE AND FEASTING, FLOWERS AND RITUALS OF PROTECTION, BELTANE CELEBRATIONS MARK THE LONG-AWAITED START OF SUMMER AND THE WARM MONTHS TO FOLLOW

WORDS Willow Winsham

Beltane is the cross quarter day of the year celebrated on 1 May, also popularly known as May Day. This seasonal festival marks the beginning of summer, and is one of the most important and widely celebrated festivals of the Wheel of the Year.

Both historically and today, fire and Beltane go hand in hand. Bonfires have been a central part of Beltane celebrations for centuries past, both in celebration and ritual. One such ritual, recorded in Irish sources from the 10th century, involves leading cattle through or round lit bonfires amidst incantations, in the belief that this would bring protection for the months to come. It has also been considered lucky to walk around or jump over the bonfire. Bonfires feature prominently in celebrations of Beltane today, and it is still considered lucky to jump over the Beltane bonfire. Another important aspect of Beltane celebration is feasting, with offerings made to the spirits or gods for a fertile and prosperous summer ahead.

Although Belanus, 'The Shining One', a Sun god of Celtic origin, is often said to be associated with Beltane, as is Bel, the protector and father god, there is little historical evidence for these deities being a part of earlier celebrations. 'Bel' might, in fact, refer to a small gap or passage, while 'tane' or 'taine' is Old Irish for 'fire'.

For Beltane, windows and doors were decorated with May flowers. These were not mere ornament however, for those points of entry were believed to need most protection in a household. The hanging of boughs over doorways was also believed to bring good milk production for cows. It is also at Beltane that we see such familiar traditions as maypole dancing, the decorating of may bushes, and the crowning of the May Queen.

The veil between the worlds is said to be thin at Beltane. Due to this, there are many superstitions and traditions linked with May Day and May Eve. The first dew of Beltane is said to have magical qualities, guaranteeing those who bathe in it a perfect complexion.

The popularity of Beltane slowly declined, however, and by the mid 20th century was no longer widely celebrated. There has since been a cultural revival in some areas, with old and new practices coming together into modern celebrations of Beltane as observed by Pagans today.

For those who rise early there is magic to be found in May Day dew; washing in it will ensure a fresh, clear complexion

> **Bonfires feature prominently in celebrations of Beltane today**

BELTANE

Fire, known for its protective and cleansing properties, is central to celebrations of Beltane, both past and present

DID YOU KNOW...
Beltane festivities are often associated with love spells and fertility rites as well as cleansing fire and protection rituals

GREEN WITCHCRAFT

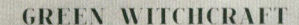

Litha

THE MIDSUMMER FESTIVAL LITHA CELEBRATES THE POWER OF THE SUN AND THE CONQUEST OF NIGHT, YET HINTS AT THE DARKNESS TO COME

WORDS Ben Gazur

The summer solstice has always been a traditional focal point of the year. On 21 or 22 June, in the northern hemisphere, the Sun reaches the end of its seasonal wanderings. No day is longer and no night is shorter. For Pagans this day is marked by the festival of Litha and represents the triumph of light over darkness.

Throughout northern Europe the day has been traditionally marked by huge bonfires whose blazes further diminish the night. Those who leapt through the flames, without mishap, were considered to have been blessed for the coming year. In the past midsummer was celebrated by setting fire to a wooden wheel representing the Sun and rolling it down a hill into a lake. This may reflect the dual nature of the summer solstice, in that while it is the longest day it also presages the return of winter, as from then on the days will become ever shorter. Christians incorporated midsummer festivities into their calendar by joining them to the feast of Saint John.

From the ancient veneration of midsummer in the old religions, the celebration of Litha has developed in modern Paganism. Traditionally the Oak King is thought to be at his strongest, with his brother the Holly King at his lowest ebb. To celebrate the victory of the Oak King, oak trees can be decorated with colourful scraps of cloth. With all the riches of the summer available Litha is a time of feasting on nature's delights like honey. It is also a time of purification

LITHA

Midsummer celebrations often incorporate fire to help drive back the night even further and extend the victory of the Sun

> **Many consider it to be a day full of magic**

DID YOU KNOW...
Midsummer celebrates both the longest day of the sun and the awareness that the days will now begin to shorten

The summer solstice, also called Litha, is a time of pilgrimage for modern Pagans to ancient sites like Stonehenge

when the dangers of the coming months can be washed away in wild bodies of water.

There are many ways to observe Litha, and as many consider it to be a day full of magic, there are many spells and rituals that can be performed then. In the day the light of the Sun may be used to gather herbs at their most potent. At night the fires that are set are thought to ward away evil as well as darkness. Folklore gives us many rites to try around these fires. Wishes can be 'given to a pebble' – whisper a wish to a stone in your hand as you walk three times around the fire and then toss it in if you want your wish to come true. Even the cold ashes of a Litha bonfire have power if they are used to create a magical talisman.

GREEN WITCHCRAFT

Lughnasadh

THE FIRST OF THREE HARVEST FESTIVALS, LUGHNASADH OR LAMMAS FOCUSES ON THE FIRST WHEAT OF THE YEAR, AND THE BREAD MADE FROM IT

WORDS Ben Gazur

Lughnasadh, also known as Lammas, marks the mid-point between summer and autumn and is the first of three harvest festival in the Pagan year. Falling around the beginning of August (or February in the southern hemisphere) it coincides with the first fruits of the harvest being brought in. In agrarian societies the time before the first harvest would have been one of dwindling supplies as they waited for the grain to ripen. After the backbreaking work of harvest, a celebration of the bounty was only natural.

Lughnasadh takes its name from the Irish god Lugh, who is said to have instituted the festival in honour of his foster-mother Tailtiu. Tailtiu spent her life, literally, clearing Ireland to make it suitable for agriculture. At the end of her labours she dropped dead, so Lugh decided to celebrate her efforts when the first harvest came each year. Lughnasadh shows how the cycle of life, death, harvesting, and sowing are all bound together, with one year's crop being the next year's seed.

Lammas, meaning Loaf Mass, was the time in England when the first wheat was cut and turned into bread. The first loaf of the year was a sacred item and consecrated. An Anglo-Saxon ritual saw this bread torn into quarters and placed in the corners of a barn to protect the rest of the harvest. Christian tradition also saw the importance of the day, and loaves would be blessed by priests and marked with symbols.

Today Lammas and Lughnasadh are celebrated by Wiccans and other Pagans in many ways. As with other Sabbats in the Wheel of the Year, bonfires are popular. Here they mirror the Sun that has made the plants grow and give thanks, hopefully, for the good weather that accompanies the harvest. The baking of a special loaf is often performed and it may be shaped into the figure of a god, or of sheaves of wheat. Ritually eating the god brings the power of the harvest within the worshipper. The last stalks of wheat harvested are made into corn dollies.

Other rites may prove more powerful at Lammas. Gerald Gardner and other witches used this day to perform a ritual in 1940 that was supposed to raise a 'cone of power' over Britain and stop the Nazis invading. Not all gatherings have such lofty aims and many Pagans meet at Lammas to dance, sing, and feast to welcome back another successful year.

> **Gerald Gardner used this day in 1940 to perform a ritual to stop the Nazis invading Britain**

The festival of Lughnasadh commemorates the goddess Tailtiu's role in making the land good for agriculture

74

LUGHNASADH

DID YOU KNOW...
The first loaf made from the harvested wheat is sacred to the gods of the harvest and used in many rituals

The first harvest represents the gifts of Mother Nature brought forth by the hard work of humanity

GREEN WITCHCRAFT

Mabon

AT THE AUTUMNAL EQUINOX THE NIGHTS BECOME LONGER THAN THE DAYS, AND PEOPLE MUST PREPARE FOR THE DARK TIMES AHEAD

WORDS Ben Gazur

The autumnal equinox, when day and night are of equal length, is a turning point in the year. Mabon is the day that begins the descent into winter as night overtakes day. Yet it is also a celebration as the second harvest festival in the Pagan calendar as nature continues to offer up its treasures. With the main harvest coming to an end, the equinox was a time of change. Farm labourers would be released from their contracts and new work sought. The whole year ahead might depend on your luck at this time.

The equinox was a key time of year for our ancestors, who had to work by daylight alone. As the sun lessened there were fewer hours in the day in which to store away food for the hard winter ahead. Many cultures marked the autumnal equinox, with many ancient sites being built so as to align with the rising Sun on those days. Pagans today will often gather at such sites to worship. While nothing can be done to stop the seasonal disappearance of the Sun, Pagans offer up praise for its abundance and calls for it to return in spring. The rite acknowledges the seasonal nature of sunlight, growth and the Earth.

The ancient pagans of Greece and Rome associated the Autumnal Equinox with the tale of Demeter and Persephone (Ceres and Proserpina to the Romans). Demeter was the fertility goddess responsible for the natural world and Persephone was her daughter. When the god of the dead stole Persephone away, Demeter in her grief stopped all living things from growing and winter set in. To save the Earth it was decreed that Persephone should spend half the year in Hades and half with her mother. While Persephone is in the realm of the living Demeter is happy and summer prevails, but the autumnal equinox marked her passage to the underworld.

To some Pagans the equinox is called Mabon and is a time to think on the delicate balance of life. Others see the ripening of grapes as a reason to celebrate the loosening powers of wine. Those wishing to see the future may wish to cut open an apple horizontally. The seeds inside form a pentagram and in the whorls of flesh around them can be read symbols of your fortune. The Harvest Moon, the full Moon closest to the equinox, is considered by some to be especially powerful.

MABON

> "The whole year ahead might depend on your luck at this time"

Mabon falls at the height of the harvest and is a time to enjoy the riches of the field

Long recognised in the ancient world as a special day, the autumnal equinox is still celebrated by Pagans today at spiritually potent sites

DID YOU KNOW...
The name 'Mabon' comes from the legend of an Arthurian knight, who was the son of a Welsh Earth Mother goddess

GREEN WITCHCRAFT

Samhain

HALLOWEEN MAY HAVE LARGELY REPLACED IT, BUT SAMHAIN IS STILL ONE OF THE MOST IMPORTANT FESTIVALS IN THE PAGAN YEAR

words Ben Gazur

Samhain, falling on 31 October, is the last of the three harvest festivals for Pagans. It also marks the true beginning of winter and was seen as a day of the dead. Several Neolithic tombs were constructed in such a way that the light of sunrise on Samhain would illuminate the interior. The Christian Allhallowtide held on the same day may preserve this association with the dead, as its ringing of church bells is thought to provide comfort to the departed.

The early descriptions of Samhain in Irish literature show it as a time to end farming and warfare and to gather families and tribes together to survive the winter. In the cold nights there was much drinking and tale-telling to pass the time. Samhain itself was a time of potential danger, as the fairies would open their mounds and it was possible for the dead to return from the spirit realm. Samhain was the time when cattle and other livestock were slaughtered and preserved for winter and it may have been a time that was associated with sacrifices.

On Samhain the fire in the hearth was allowed to burn out while people worked in the fields. That night bonfires were lit to ward off evil and fire was taken from these to relight the home fires. The smoke from the great fires was thought to be protective. Sometimes two fires were lit and villagers and livestock would pass between them.

Today bonfires are still lit at Samhain. Major cities such as Edinburgh see large processions of people carrying flaming torches alongside drums and music. Traditionally the festivities of Samhain could be accompanied by dressing up and disguise. Boys would sometimes go from house to house to beg wood to be added to the communal fire. To light the way revellers carved lanterns from turnips and wurzels. It is easy to see how Samhain influenced the later traditions of Halloween, which many people celebrate today.

For modern Pagans, Samhain is both a time to remember the dead and to celebrate. Feasts are often held as a way of offering hospitality to the deceased. You may want to bake a batch of soul cakes to offer to the poor. It is also a time to introduce newborns to the community. Samhain can be the proper moment to reflect on things that have ended in the past year, as well as the hopes for what may come in the next.

DID YOU KNOW...
The boundaries between the human world and those of the fairies and the dead are thought to grow thin and permeable at Samhain

SAMHAIN

Samhain brings Pagans together to celebrate life and death as they remember those who have passed on

Samhain is a liminal time when the boundaries between the living, dead, and fairy realms are thin. Many tombs align with the sun on Samhain

79

GREEN WITCHCRAFT

Seasons, Signs and Decans

HARMONISING WITH MOTHER NATURE MEANS EMBRACING HER NATURAL RHYTHMS, AND OFTEN THIS MEANS NOT LOOKING DOWN TOWARDS THE EARTH, BUT UP TOWARDS THE SKY...

WORDS Alice Pattillo

SEASONS, SIGNS & DECANS

Seasons

Embracing and following the seasonal rhythm where you are is a vital part of green witchcraft

Not all of the world recognises four seasons. Many temperate regions acknowledge six ecological seasons that split spring and summer into two based on the characteristics of wildlife and plants. Similarly, six seasons are recognised in the traditional Hindu calendar and each one lasts two months. Starting in mid-March, the seasonal calender is as follows: Vasanta (spring), Grishma (summer), Varsha (monsoon), Sharada (autumn), Hemanta (early winter or late autumn) and Shishira (prevernal or late winter).

Many tropical regions observe two seasons: Wet (also known as Rainy or Monsoon season) and Dry. Thailand recognises three seasons: Hot, Cold and Rainy. Meanwhile, the Japanese traditional calendar recognises a whopping 24 major seasonal divisions and 72 micro seasons that last around five days each.

Wherever you are in the world, attuning yourself to its seasonal rhythms will help you to understand the life cycle of the plants and trees around you and how that relates to your green witch practise. We've focused primarily on the northern hemisphere here, but if you're in the southern hemisphere then the solstices and equinoxes will be reversed, and spring zodiac signs appear in autumn.

SPRING

Spring is associated with growth, fertility, fire and light. Its the beginning of a new cycle and a time of transition, marking the return of the Sun. In the northern hemisphere, spring begins at the vernal equinox (around March 21) also known as Ostara, although Celtic tradition marks its start at Imbolc (February 1).

SUMMER

Summer is associated with abundance, growth and masculine solar energy; its symbols include flowers, fire, warmth, strength and light. It is also the start of the harvest. Summer begins either at May Day (Beltane) or at the Summer Solstice (Midsummer), depending on which feels right for you.

WINTER

Winter is the coldest season, associated with darkness, ice, snow, death, rest and regeneration. The veil between worlds is at its thinnest at this time – between Samhain (Halloween, October 31) through to Winter Solstice (Yule, December 21) where the day is shortest and the night is longest. Historically, it was a dangerous time when disease and death reached their peak. It's a time to let go and restore your energy.

AUTUMN

Autumn is associated with the harvest, maturity, renewal, introspection, creativity and change. Symbols include baskets, feasts, apples and acorns. Autumn traditionally began with Lammas (around August 1), with the autumnal equinox, also known as Mabon, marking the harvest festival (around September 21). It's a time to prepare for hibernation and preparation for the coming winter.

DID YOU KNOW…

On the spring and autumn equinoxes, day and night are of roughly equal length across the planet, whereas on the solstices, one is significantly longer than the other

GREEN WITCHCRAFT

Zodiac Signs

The constellation that the sun and moon are moving through can make a difference to how your garden grows

The zodiac is a belt of 12 constellations that extends approximately eight degrees north and eight degrees south of the Earth's orbital plane around the sun. The zodiac is the sun's apparent path throughout the year, as seen from the Earth, and the orbital pathways of the moon and major planets are all within the zodiac belt. In Western astrology, as the sun appears to pass through the zodiac it passes through its 12 different constellations, each of which occupies 30 degrees of the full 360 degree belt. It takes a year for the sun to pass through all of the constellations. The moon, however, is much quicker. Each sign has advantages for practitioners of green witchcraft, so keep an eye on the sky for more than just rain…

Aries
MAR 21 - APR 19

Aries is a fire sign ruled by Mars, so when the sun or moon are passing through it, it's a good time to get aggressive: weed, prune, and discourage unwelcome garden pests!

Taurus
APR 20 - MAY 20

Taurus is an earth sign, so when the sun or moon are passing through this fertile sign, it's a great time to plant seeds, prick out seedlings or pot on young plants. It's especially good for root crops like potatoes, carrots and radishes. Also, roses are sacred to its ruler, Venus.

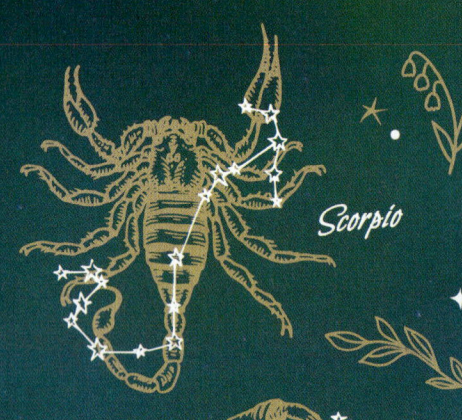

Gemini
MAY 21 - JUN 20

Air sign Gemini is considered a barren sign — if the sun or moon are in the sign of the Twins then it's not a good time for planting. Its dry mercurial energy though makes it great for harvesting, particularly for grains or seeds that you plan to store for some time.

Cancer
JUN 21 - JUL 22

Water sign Cancer is considered one of the best signs for plant fertility and growth, so if the sun or moon are in the Crab, then it's time to plant seeds and nourish young plants with mulch or compost.

Leo
JUL 23 - AUG 22

Like Aries, Leo is a barren fire sign, so if the sun or moon are here then it's best to stick to pruning, weeding, cutting back and pest control, rather than planting seeds or young plants.

Scorpio

Aquarius

Taurus

Virgo
AUG 23 - SEP 22

Virgo is an earth sign, but unlike its other earthy companions, it's a barren one. When the sun or moon are in this orderly, rigorous sign, it's a good time to neaten things up, especially if you have plants you want to train into shapes.

DID YOU KNOW…

The sun is not the only celestial body to pass through the zodiac — the moon and the planets do too. When you hear an astrologer talking about 'astral weather', it's this they're referring to

SEASONS, SIGNS & DECANS

Libra
SEP 23 – OCT 22

Libra is an air sign and when the sun or moon are passing through it, it's a good time to pick flowers, especially if you plan on drying or preserving them. It's not the worst time to plant seeds, but not the best either.

Scorpio
OCT 23 – NOV 21

As a water sign, when the sun or moon is in Scorpio it's a great time for sowing seeds and potting out smaller plants, especially in rich soil or compost. Pruning during this time will also help your plants to put on lush new growth.

Sagittarius
NOV 22 – DEC 21

Another barren fire sign, when the sun or moon is in Sagittarius, it's a good time to chop and weed. If you prune plants when the moon is in Sagittarius, they'll grow more slowly – great for dealing with fast growers like fig or bramble.

Capricorn
DEC 22 – JAN 19

When the sun or moon are in earth sign Capricorn, it's a reasonably good time to sow seeds and plant seedlings. Pruning plants, trees and shrubs during this time will help them to put on healthy new growth.

Aquarius
JAN 20 – FEB 18

Air sign Aquarius isn't a great time for sowing or planting, but great for harvesting crops that will go into storage. It's also good for general tidying up and other gardening chores.

Pisces
FEB 19 – MAR 20

When the sun or moon is in the water sign of the Fish, it's a great time for sowing, planting and fertilising all kinds of plants, as well as potting into bigger pots or out into the earth of a prepared garden bed.

GREEN WITCHCRAFT

Decans

Each zodiac sign has three distinct subdivisions that have subtly different influences affecting them

> They are sub-ruled by another sign with the same element

Each sign of the zodiac can be further split into three subdivisions called decans. These are 10 degree (day) splits within each sign, the second two of which are sub-ruled by another sign with the same element, but a different ruling planet. The first ten degrees of a sign is ruled by the same sign, the second ten degrees by the next sign of the same element, and the third ten degrees by the third sign. When the moon is passing through Cancer, for example, Cancer I, ruled by Cancer's native ruler the moon, is a good time to perform Cancer's gardening activities. Cancer II is a Scorpio decan, so it's not quite so good. But Cancer III is a Pisces decan, meaning you get the best of both gardening worlds and can take advantage of both Pisces and Cancer's fertile planting energies!

DID YOU KNOW?
Decans apply to every aspect of your chart. The moon and planets also pass through the zodiac and therefore their decans. This can add depth and additional meaning to astrological magic

	Aries Mar21-Apr20	Taurus Apr21-May20	Gemini May21-Jun20
DECAN I			
DEGREES	0°-10°	0°-10°	0°-10°
DATES	Mar 21-30	Apr 20-29	May 21-30
RULING SIGN	Aries	Taurus	Gemini
RULING PLANET	Mars	Venus	Mercury
DECAN II			
DEGREES	11°-20°	11°-20°	11°-20°
DATES	Apr 1-9	Apr 30-May 9	May 31-Jun 9
RULING SIGN	Leo	Virgo	Libra
RULING PLANET	Sun	Mercury	Venus
DECAN III			
DEGREES	21°-30°	21°-30°	21°-30°
DATES	Apr 10-19	May 10-20	Jun 10-20
RULING SIGN	Sagittarius	Capricorn	Aquarius
RULING PLANET	Jupiter	Saturn	Uranus

SEASONS, SIGNS & DECANS

Cancer	Leo	Virgo	Libra	Scorpio	Sagittarius	Capricorn	Aquarius	Pisces
Jun21-Jul22	Jul23-Aug22	Aug23-Sep22	Sep23-Oct22	Oct23-Nov22	Nov23-Dec21	Dec22-Jan19	Jan20-Feb19	Feb20-Mar20
0°-10°	0°-10°	0°-10°	0°-10°	0°-10°	0°-10°	0°-10°	0°-10°	0°-10°
Jun 21-30	Jul 23-Aug 1	Aug 23-Sep 1	Sep 23-Oct 2	Oct 23-Nov 1	Nov 22-Dec 1	Dec 22-31	Jan 20-29	Feb 19-29
Cancer	Leo	Virgo	Libra	Scorpio	Sagittarius	Capricorn	Aquarius	Pisces
Moon	Sun	Mercury	Venus	Pluto	Jupiter	Saturn	Uranus	Neptune
11°-20°	11°-20°	11°-20°	11°-20°	11°-20°	11°-20°	11°-20°	11°-20°	11°-20°
Jul 1-10	Aug 2-11	Sep 2-11	Oct 3-12	Nov 2-11	Dec 2-11	Jan 1-10	Jan 30-Feb 8	Mar 1-10
Scorpio	Sagittarius	Capricorn	Aquarius	Pisces	Aries	Taurus	Gemini	Cancer
Pluto	Jupiter	Saturn	Uranus	Neptune	Mars	Venus	Mercury	Moon
21°-30°	21°-30°	21°-30°	21°-30°	21°-30°	21°-30°	21°-30°	21°-30°	21°-30°
Jul 11-22	Aug 12-22	Sep 12-22	Oct 13-22	Nov 12-21	Dec 12-21	Jan 11-19	Feb 9-18	Mar 11-20
Pisces	Aries	Taurus	Gemini	Cancer	Leo	Virgo	Libra	Scorpio
Neptune	Mars	Venus	Mercury	Moon	Sun	Mercury	Venus	Pluto
♋	♌	♍	♎	♏	♐	♑	♒	♓

GREEN WITCHCRAFT

Gardening with the Moon

HOW GETTING IN TUNE WITH THE MOON CAN HELP YOU TO CREATE A BEAUTIFUL GARDEN

WORDS Sally Trotman

Planting by the moon phases can have a profound impact on the health, happiness, and wellbeing of plants. By observing the connection between the moon and the Earth, it is possible to tap into the moon's energy to achieve the best gardening results. Aligning gardening activities with the phases of the moon allows you to tap into the natural cycles of growth. It is believed that the gravitational pull of the moon affects the flow of sap and energy within plants, influencing their overall development.

By following the monthly rhythm of the moon, you will see that your plants are becoming more robust, vibrant and resilient. Flowers bloom more profusely, fruits ripen with greater flavour and sweetness, and seeds develop to their full potential. This in turn leads to bountiful harvests, and an abundance of seeds for future plantings. It is even believed that by planting in tune with the moon, these plants experience improved disease resistance, reduced pest infestations, and increased tolerance to adverse weather conditions. By working in harmony with the moon's energy, an optimal environment is created for plants to thrive. Whilst scientific evidence supporting the direct influence of the moon's phases on plant growth remains limited, immense satisfaction and a deep sense of connection can be derived from practicing gardening with the moon. It is a way to honour ancient wisdom, cultivate mindfulness, and develop a profound bond with nature. Gardening with the moon creates a beautiful dance between the earth and the sky, which in turn can lead to a more abundant garden!

> **Tap into the moon's energy to achieve the best gardening results**

GARDENING WITH THE MOON

Moon Phases

Discover the moon's phases and what they're best for

NEW MOON

During the new moon phase, focus on planning, soil preparation, and maintenance tasks. Avoid planting or sowing seeds, as the energy is low and growth potential is limited.

WAXING CRESCENT

Whilst the moon is in the waxing crescent phase, it is favourable to plant above-ground crops. The energy is increasing, which will support healthy leafy growth.

FIRST QUARTER

During the first quarter moon phase, focus on planting, especially leafy vegetables and annual flowers. The energy is increasing, supporting growth and establishment.

WAXING GIBBOUS

Whilst at the waxing gibbous moon phase, this is a good time for maintenance tasks, such as weeding, fertilising, and pruning. Avoid major planting activities now.

FULL MOON

During the full moon, focus on harvesting crops especially those that bear fruit above ground. It is a good time to appreciate the beauty of your garden.

WANING GIBBOUS

The waning gibbous phase of the moon is favourable for pruning, thinning, and transplanting. Avoid planting new crops as the energy is decreasing.

LAST QUARTER

During the last quarter of the moon, focus on weeding, pest control, and any general garden clean up. Avoid planting and prepare for the next cycle.

WANING CRESCENT

Prioritise soil enrichment and composting during the waning crescent moon. Avoid major planting activities and focus on restorative tasks to prepare for the next lunar cycle.

DID YOU KNOW...
When looking at the moon, if the illuminated curve of the moon is on the right side, it is waxing. When on the left side, it is waning

GREEN WITCHCRAFT

" Moon signs are an important aspect of astrology

DID YOU KNOW…

Planting on the New Moon and the quarter days themselves is generally not advised when gardening. It is better to focus on planning, preparation and other non-planting activities during these phases

Moon Signs & Best Days

The moon moves through the zodiac, making some days better for gardening tasks than others

Moon signs are an important aspect of astrology, and influence various areas of life, including gardening activities. In astrology, the moon moves through different zodiac signs approximately every 2.5 days, creating a cycle of lunar energy that can affect the success of gardening endeavours. Understanding moon signs and their influence on gardening can help to optimise planting, pruning and harvesting. Certain zodiac signs are considered barren for gardening activities. When the moon is in these signs, it is less favourable for planting, or sowing seeds. Aries is a fire sign, associated with heat and dryness. It is considered a barren sign for planting, so it is best to avoid transplanting during this moon sign. Gemini is an air sign, known for its changeability. It is also considered a barren sign for planting leafy vegetables or flowers. When the moon is in the other air signs such as Libra or Aquarius, focus on pruning, grafting and tending to flowers. Avoid planting or sowing seeds during this time. More fruitful moon signs to plant under are Taurus, Cancer, Virgo, Scorpio and Capricorn. Taurus is an earth sign, which is associated with stability and fertility. The best crops to plant during this moon sign are root crops and plants that bear fruit below the ground. Virgo and Capricorn are also earth signs. Virgo is a practical and organised sign, so planting during this moon phase will promote healthy and strong roots. Planting whilst the moon is in Capricorn is beneficial for slow-growing crops and plants that require strong foundations. This is a steady sign and patience pays here! Cancer is a water sign, and planting during this moon sign is beneficial for leafy greens, and plants that require plenty of water. Nurture these plants as Cancer responds to care and attention. As Scorpio is a water sign that is associated with transformation, planting during this moon phase will enhance the growth of root crops and plants that bear fruit above the ground. It is important to take other factors into consideration when gardening, such as climate, local soil conditions and individual plant needs, which also play a part in gardening success. It is helpful to consider these factors in conjunction with planting with the moon signs for the best outcomes. By aligning gardening activities with the corresponding moon signs, you can work in harmony with the natural rhythms, potentially enhancing plant growth, and overall garden productivity.

WHY NOT TRY...

Planting above-ground crops during the waxing moon phase is favourable as this period promotes leafy growth. Planting below-ground crops during the waning moon phase is helpful to enhance root development and yield healthier harvests

GREEN WITCHCRAFT

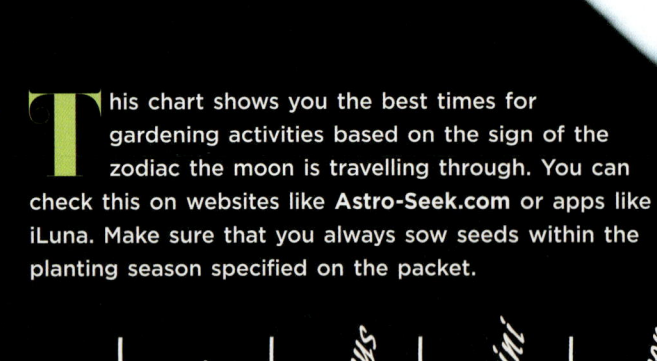

Best

This chart shows you the best times for gardening activities based on the sign of the zodiac the moon is travelling through. You can check this on websites like **Astro-Seek.com** or apps like iLuna. Make sure that you always sow seeds within the planting season specified on the packet.

	Aries	Taurus	Gemini	Cancer	Leo	Virgo	Libra
PLANT SEEDS *above ground plants*		✦		✦✦✦			✦✦
PLANT SEEDS *root plants*		✦✦✦	✦		✦	✦✦✦	✦✦
GRAFT or POLLINATE	✦	✦✦✦	✦✦✦	✦			✦✦✦
PRUNE to *ENCOURAGE* NEW GROWTH	✦✦✦				✦✦✦		
PRUNE to *DISCOURAGE* NEW GROWTH		✦✦		✦			
WEEDING	✦✦		✦✦	✦✦✦		✦✦	✦✦
HARVEST *above ground plants*	✦✦	✦✦		✦✦✦	✦	✦✦	
HARVEST *below ground plants*		✦✦	✦				✦✦
PICK FRUIT	✦	✦✦		✦✦✦✦	✦✦		
DRY HERBS & VEGETABLES			✦✦			✦✦✦	
CAN, PICKLE & PRESERVE FRUIT & VEGETABLES		✦✦✦	✦✦		✦✦		✦
BAKING		✦✦✦		✦✦✦		✦✦✦	✦✦✦

Days

GARDENING WITH THE MOON

Key

★★★ An excellent time for this activity

★★ A good time for this activity

★ An okay time for this activity

> More fruitful moon signs to plant under are Taurus, Cancer, Virgo, Scorpio and Capricorn

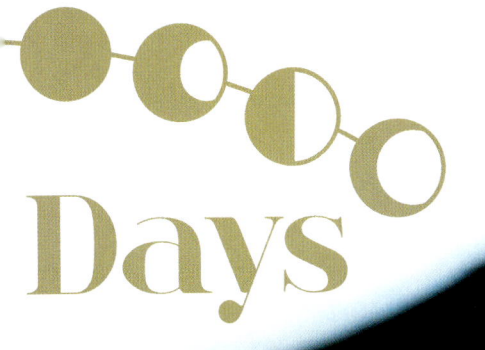

Scorpio	Sagittarius	Capricorn	Aquarius	Pisces
★	★★		★	★★
		★★★		★★
	★		★★★	
	★★★	★★★		
★★★		★★★		★★★
★★★		★	★	
	★			
★		★★		★
	★★		★	
★	★★		★★★★	
		★★★		★★
★★		★	★	★★

♏ ♐ ♑ ♒ ♓

GREEN WITCHCRAFT

The Witches Apothecary

PLANTS AND HERBAL REMEDIES ARE A POTENT
SOURCE OF MEDICINE AND MAGIC

WORDS *Alice Pattillo*

Witchcraft and herbs are eternally entwined. In ancient Greece, Pliny wrote of local wise women who worshipped the goddess Hecate. Her followers included the mythical witches Circe and Medea, who used herbal medicines to both cure and kill. Medieval wise women were skilled healers and plant experts who could identify and administer natural pharmaceuticals, and had expertise that threatened the emerging male-dominated institution of modern medicine, leading to church-encouraged propaganda and kicking off centuries of witch hunts.

Herbalism is at the core of modern medicine, too. Willow bark was used for centuries to treat aches and pains, for fever reduction and relief of menstrual cramps. Its active ingredient, salicylic acid has since been replicated as aspirin and is taken medicinally. What's more, the same ingredient is a powerful skin exfoliant for a glowing, radiant complexion. Another potent painkiller is morphine, derived from opium poppies. And we are still discovering more therapeutic ingredients and cures from plants and herbs. In the 1950s, galantamine was first extracted from snowdrops and is now aiding Alzheimer's sufferers.

While witches are not pharmacists (although some may have a degree in it!), using safe herbs and herbal remedies is one of the backbones of green witches' practice.

DID YOU KNOW…

Bach's Flower Remedies are a 20th-century form of homeopathy developed from exclusively flower material – particularly petals – that are believed to contain the energetic nature of the flower mixed in a solution of water and brandy

APOTHECARY

Herbal Remedies

Humans have been using plants and their extracts to ease pain, tend to skin complaints, treat viruses and infections, and heighten their senses for millennia. Many herbs and plants have numerous natural healing properties when consumed or applied topically, from being antibacterial, antiviral, antimicrobial and antifungal to anti-inflammatory, antiseptic, antioxidant, anticoagulant and expectorant.

Herbalism also remains popular and readily available in the form of raw herbal teas, tinctures (dilute), powders, tablets and capsules, and ointments containing essential oils. The majority of our modern herbal remedies are derived from either European and North American traditions and plants (Western herbal medicine), traditional Chinese medicine or Indian Ayurvedic medicine. Many herbs are perfectly safe for human consumption in their raw fresh and dried forms and less potent than synthetic drugs. However, it is important to keep in mind that many others are not, and while in their natural state many of the active ingredients within plants are unreliable and often contain toxins – hence why they are separated, synthesised and put through years of stringent testing before they are released to the masses via mainstream medicine. Herbal medicine is a complementary therapy and not a replacement for proper medical care. Don't reject mainstream medication in favour of herbal remedies, and remember that this guide is not medical advice. Ensure you talk to a doctor before trying anything – contraindications and side effects exist with herbs just as with any other pharmaceuticals – and seek a licensed herbal practitioner.

A selection of antique preserved herbal remedies

Images Getty Images, Øyvind Holmstad/CC BY-SA 3.0 (antique preserved herbal remedies)

Essential Herbs

CHAMOMILE

One of the most ancient herbal remedies, chamomile soothes stomach pains, headaches and anxiety. As well as calming nerves, chamomile is associated with the sun, purification and protection. It promotes a feeling of harmony and happiness, peace and healing, and encourages prosperity and luck.

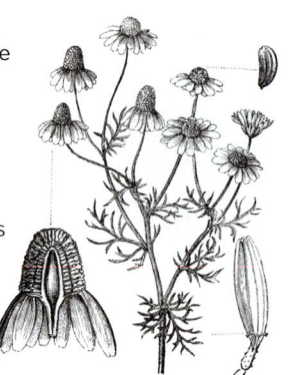

YARROW

Used in healing ointments for soft tissue injuries and in tea to dispel depression, yarrow is also effective against fevers. As well as being a healing herb, yarrow promotes courage and self-esteem. Hang a sprig over your bed for a passionate partnership or bathe with it to encourage psychic abilities.

CLARY SAGE

Clary sage, just like any sage, is associated with clarity and purification. Its oestrogen-like effects make it ideal for menstrual complaints and issues associated with the menopause. Clary sage holds the energy of the full moon, making it excellent for meditation, increasing intuition, lucid dreaming, concentration and altered states of consciousness.

MUGWORT

Mentioned in the Anglo Saxon Nine Herbs Charm, mugwort has been used since at least the Iron Age for medicine, magic and food. An effective insect repellent, mugwort also aids sleeplessness and dream magic. Use it to invoke prophetic dreams, astral travel and divination, as well as a powerful protection and cleansing herb.

VERVAIN (VERBENA)

Associated with the divine and supernatural since ancient times, its nicknames have included "Tears of Isis", "Holy Herb" and "Devil's Bane". It has antiseptic qualities, calms headaches, relaxes and eases stress. Magically, it is used to protect against curses, aid divination, inspire love and tranquillity, and encourage success and abundance.

VALERIAN

Used in herbalism for centuries, valerian is a natural sedative and excellent for treating anxiety. A potent protective herb, the Greeks hung it in their homes to ward off evil forces as well as facilitating journeys between realms, truth and connection.

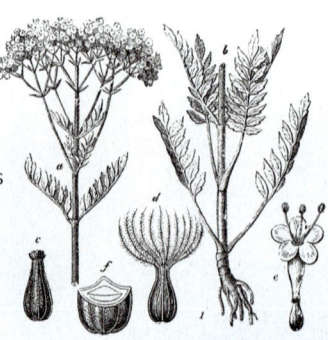

LAVENDER

A powerfully protective and cleansing herb, lavender was historically used to ward away evil spirits in churches, as well as disinfect in the form of soaps. Leave a sprig beside your bed to attract a lover, put some under your pillow or in a tea to banish insomnia.

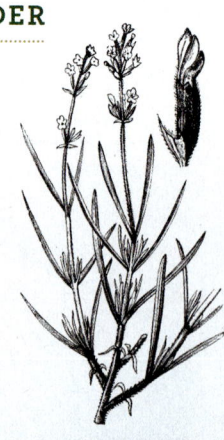

APOTHECARY

An old homeopathic dilution of Rhus toxicodendron, aka Poison Ivy

WITCH HAZEL

Witch hazel blooms in winter and its branches were used for dowsing for water, making it excellent for divination, discovery and journeying – in this world and the next. Witch hazel is also a blood flow balancer and excellent skin healer – its anti-inflammatory and antiseptic qualities make it perfect for helping treat minor skin complaints.

ROSEMARY

A kitchen essential, rosemary is also full of medicinal and magical properties. Sacred to the ancients, it is often linked to burial rites and remembrance. In one Spanish fairytale, rosemary is used to restore memory and its magical associations include memory, wisdom, healing and protection. Fantastic as a skin and hair tonic, the herb will soothe an itchy scalp, while when drunk in tea, it can aid headaches.

PEPPERMINT

Peppermint has been used to aid digestive disorders, spasms and flavour food since ancient times. Peppermint is excellent for keeping pests away, freshening up your breath, toning and refreshing your skin and is a natural stimulant. It purifies and renews, and will attract passion into your love life.

> **Peppermint is excellent for keeping pests away and freshening up your breath**

Homeopathy

Homeopathy is a form of alternative medicine developed in Germany in the 18th century by physician Samuel Hahnemann. Its philosophy is that "like cures like", i.e., that diseases can be cured by substances that produce similar symptoms in an otherwise healthy person. However, Hahnemann believed that large doses of the substances would only aggravate illnesses, so instead opted for heavy dilutions – developing the quintamillesimal (Q) scale which diluted the substance 1 part to 50,000 dilute (usually water, alcohol or sugar). The dilute substance itself is so heavily diluted that it is scientifically indistinguishable from the original dilute itself. However, Hahnemann believed that the dilution process preserved the "spirit-like medicinal powers" of the substance while removing its harmful effects.

Hahnemann's text, The *Organon of the Healing Art*, published in 1810, still informs modern-day homeopathy and introduces the concept of miasms. Miasms are the "infectious principles" underlying diseases that, according to Hahnemann, are suppressed by conventional medicines. Modern medicines, he said, simply treated the symptoms and not the cause. Modern homeopaths use animal, plant, mineral and synthetic substances in their preparations, including snake venom, arsenic, opium and salts and often prescribe pills, typically made of sugars, upon which a drop of their dilute liquid is applied and left to evaporate.

GREEN WITCHCRAFT

Kitchen Craft

WITCHES ARE OFTEN DEPICTED IN THE HEARTH OF THEIR HOMES AND FOR GOOD REASON – IT IS WHERE THEIR LIFE-GIVING FIRE KEEPS THEIR CAULDRONS COOKING AND THE MAGIC BREWING

WORDS Alice Pattillo

Domestic Deities

The gods of hearth and home watch over food, family and folk traditions

In ancient Greek myth, the goddess Hestia forever tended to the hearth on Mount Olympus. She was the goddess of domesticity, the family, home and state. Hestia's Roman equivalent, Vesta, had a temple in the heart of Rome. Entry was only permitted to her Vestal Virgins – priestesses who prepared flour and salt and tended to her sacred fire. She was celebrated with the festival Vestalia, one of the most important events of the Roman calendar. To Vesta, donkeys were sacred and the animals would be adorned with bread and flowers in her honour. Both Hestia and Vesta are virgin fire goddesses who had perpetual fires burning for them, and they are associated with family meals and sacrificial feasts.

In pre-Christian Ireland, the spring goddess Brigid was another fire goddess associated with the return of life, fertility and domestic animals. Spring deities are often linked to fire, food and domesticity. The Chinese kitchen god, Zao Jung, is known as the stove god. He is concerned with morality and family conduct, and his festival takes place in the spring.

In Rome, there were other deities who presided over the domestic setting – lares. In fact, many cultures didn't necessarily have a major god presiding over it, but a lesser animistic domestic deity – a house spirit or fairy-like creature. Examples of protective house spirits that survived through folklore include the Slavic domovoy, British brownies and hobgoblins, and Scandinavian nisse, tomte and tonttu.

The Vestal Virgins were selected before puberty to devote their lives to ensuring Vesta's sacred fire kept blazing and they had extraordinary rights and privileges, as long as they remained chaste

> Spring deities are often linked to fire, food and domesticity

KITCHEN CRAFT

WHY NOT TRY...

Cook with intent. As you add ingredients to the pot, think about what it is bringing to your dish in terms of magic, health and taste. Concentrate on what the intended outcome of each culinary element is

Herbs and spices are important for spellcraft and they can be utilised in food, incenses and skin-caring elixirs

Cauldrons have provided sustenance and healing to people all over the world since ancient times

Spice Up Your Life

Herbs and spices are at the heart of any witches' kitchen

Herbs, roots and spices are essential for witches' health and healing (see page 92), but they also inject magic and flavour into your dishes – or to enjoy as a therapeutic tea. St John's wort is great for soothing anxiety and fighting off troublesome entities. Chamomile is excellent for stress and tummy troubles, and can be blended with fennel for a lovely IBS-soothing tea that promotes prosperity and harmony while warding off evil spirits. Cloves can be added to baked goods and curries, and are essential for spell enhancement, spiritual healing and protection. Basil and cinnamon are perfect for attracting success and prosperity. They are also associated with energy, action, love, protection and healing. Ginger is full of potent energy that enhances your spells, helps digestion and nausea, inspires action, success and prosperity, and aids immunity. Bay leaves are associated with divination, wisdom and success. Add parsley to your dishes for power and strength, thyme for courage, nutmeg to improve psychic abilities, quell nausea and manifest success, or black pepper for protection and to increase self-esteem. Garlic is antiseptic and antibiotic, improves immunity and heart and respiratory issues. It's also a powerful banishing tool and cleanses negative energy.

Fire Burn & Cauldron Bubble

Cauldrons were pots that hung over an open fire and had been used to cook since the Bronze Age. The idea of them as spellcasting vessels developed from ancient times, when they were thought to have a practical and magical purpose. In Irish folklore, leprechauns keep their treasure in a cauldron while in Welsh mythology, the Pair Dadeni ("Cauldron of Rebirth") brings warriors back to life. Cauldrons were used in ceremonial feasts and to produce healing potions and nourishing meals, and represent the womb – which explains their association with life and rebirth. They are also typically made from cast iron, associated with banishing and purifying.

GREEN WITCHCRAFT

Making your own bread can be a magical process, and topped with honey it's nothing short of divine!

Food divination is an ancient tradition, kept alive today through Halloween customs and tea leaf reading

Moreish Magic

Numerous forms of divination and spellcraft originate in the kitchen and incorporate food staples such as tea, eggs, nuts and fruit

Often performed at Halloween, the winter solstice at Christmas, or New Year – the times of the year when the veil between this world and the next is at its thinnest – folk magic fortune-telling traditions often include tasty treats. One popular custom in Ireland was to hide objects in food, such as a ring, thimble or coin baked into a cake or bread, such as barmbrack, or a dish like colcannon. The person who finds the object is said to be married next or have good fortune. The most famous culinary form of divination is perhaps tasseomancy, or tea leaf reading. But tossing nuts into an open fire was another popular form of romantic divination, as well as apple bobbing or apple peeling.

Divination by eggs, known as oomancy, has been practised for centuries, often by reading the egg whites when dropped into hot water, in a similar fashion to molten lead divination.

In British folklore, peas could be utilised to woo your significant other, and in Scotland they performed kaling, whereby a stalk of kale blindly plucked from a field was said to reveal information about the person's future husband or wife. Onions are also ripe for the picking when it comes to prophecy. In Germany, onions are believed to be able to forecast the weather, while sprouting onions can aid in decision making.

A Recipe for Magic

Bread and honey might seem basic but they are essential ingredients for every witches' kitchen

Bread is associated with nourishment of body and soul. In Christianity, bread represents the body of Christ, and sharing. In Egypt, bread is called 'aysh' and there is an ancient proverb that says "life without aysh is not life". Bread is used as an offering and as protection from spiritual entities, such as the fae, or from evil witchcraft, and it has inspired many superstitions. The fae were said to be keen bakers and the process of baking bread is itself a ritualistic task that has been used as a form of divination and spellwork.

Honey is medicinal, used as a cough-suppressing agent and serotonin booster. It is anti-inflammatory and antibacterial and when applied topically, it helps skin conditions such as dandruff, acne and eczema. Symbolically, honey is the nectar of the gods, one of the Hindu elixirs of immortality, and is used as an offering to the goddess of beauty and love, Aphrodite. Associated with prosperity, royalty, love, fertility and community, when used in spellcraft, honey will sweeten the feelings of the object of your affection towards you.

> **Bread is also used as an offering and form of protection from spiritual entities**

KITCHEN CRAFT

Witches & Broomsticks

Broomsticks are synonymous with witches, but how has such an ordinary household item developed such supernatural connotations?

Sweeping dates back to ancient times, when people used branches and bunches of herbs to dust away ash from the fire of the hearth. It's unclear when purpose-built, natural fibre brooms were invented, but they quickly became a symbol of female domesticity. Women were the sex primarily accused of witchcraft, and illicit rumours spread that witches used broomsticks to insert "flying ointment" (thought to have been a psychedelic, hallucination-inducing concoction of herbs such as belladonna, henbane and mandrake) into their vaginas, which would allegedly cause frenzied dancing and give rise to the idea that they would ride the broomstick to cavort with the devil. Today, modern witches and Wiccans use brooms as a symbol of luck, sweeping away bad fortune and negative energy and protecting against evil.

WHY NOT TRY...
Next time you eat, take time to consider your meal. Honour the food, engage all of your senses, think about how it is sustaining you, what you are gaining from the ingredients, and how grateful you are for it

The image of the old woman with a pointed hat riding a broomstick has become the most recognisable and iconic depiction of the witch

Feeling Salty

Mentioned in folklore and used in rituals for thousands of years, salt is a magical mineral essential for every kitchen witch's pantry

Associated primarily with protection and purification, salt was a valuable commodity in ancient times and used to preserve meats. A powerful repeller of evil, it was often used to ward off evil witches and spirits. In Egypt, salt was ritualistically burned to ensure safe travel while in Slavic folklore, it was said to help determine if a child was bewitched. Use it in purification, binding and cleansing spells and to attract good luck.

Eye of Newt

Some herbs have terrifying nicknames thanks to the way they look, but don't be put off!

While many of the innocuous sounding stuff in the most infamous witches brew of all time (the recipe recited in Shakespeare's *Macbeth* by the three witches) probably are very poisonous, eye of newt is actually an essential ingredient in any witch's kitchen. Rather than being the peeper of an amphibian, it's actually mustard. Mustard seed is a traditional magical ingredient used for protection, and a dab of wholegrain mustard packs a punch in flavour too.

Images Getty Images

99

GREEN WITCHCRAFT

Hearty Party Punch

HAVING A GATHERING WHERE THE GUESTS DON'T KNOW EACH OTHER? BREAK THE ICE WITH THIS COURAGE-ENHANCING COOLER

WORDS April Madden

You'll Need...
makes 6 glasses

- 750ml bottle of sparkling white wine or non-alcoholic alternative (elderflower pressé, for example)
- 500ml soda water or sparkling mineral water
- 300g caster sugar
- 150ml water
- 1 tbsp thyme honey
- 1 tbsp dried borage leaves or 5 large fresh borage leaves from your garden
- 1 tbsp freeze-dried pansy petals or petals from 5 fresh pansies from your garden
- Fresh or canned blackberries, to serve
- Pansy ice cubes to serve (optional)
- Borage leaves and flowers, to serve (optional)

HEARTY PARTY PUNCH

This kitchen witchcraft potion is ideal when you've got a social gathering where guests don't know each other and need a little something to get the party started. It makes use of some traditional herbal properties to help people lighten up and feel less nervous. Borage (or starflower), thyme, pansies (or heartsease) and blackberries are all associated with courage. All of the ingredients can be bought dried or jarred (and in some cases fresh) online, or grown in your garden if you have one. Make sure you don't use chemical pesticides or weedkillers on any plants destined for human consumption – it's also best to avoid picking up a tray of bedding-plant pansies from your local garden centre the day before making this for the same reason.

Also, make sure to wash garden plants gently but thoroughly before using in any recipes.

Boil the water and sugar together to make a simple syrup, then add the thyme honey, borage leaves and pansy petals. Once the mixture has a thin syrupy texture, allow to cool, then strain using a fine mesh sieve or muslin cloth to leave all the plant material behind (you can compost this). Chill the syrup, soda or mineral water, and the sparkling wine or alcohol-free alternative thoroughly in the fridge.

To make pansy ice cubes, sprinkle fresh or dried pansy petals into an ice cube tray and freeze for at least four hours, preferably overnight. Use alongside regular ice cubes.

In a punchbowl or mixing bowl, combine the syrup, soda or mineral water and wine or alcohol-free alternative. Add ice cubes and blackberries to each glass and fill with the mixture. Garnish with fresh borage leaves and flowers if you have them – if you don't, a few snips from a supermarket thyme plant will also look pretty, as would pansies.

Serve, and don't forget to mingle among your guests and introduce them! This potion will give you a helping hand, but it won't do all the work for you.

WARNING
Check with your guests whether they have allergies to any of the ingredients before serving!

> Borage (or starflower), thyme, pansies (or heartsease) and blackberries are all associated with courage

GREEN WITCHCRAFT

Calm-down Cake

A TRANQUIL TEATIME TREAT TO SOOTHE OVERWROUGHT EMOTIONS AND PROMOTE REST AND RELAXATION

WORDS April Madden

WHY NOT TRY…
You could also make individual fairy cakes – just bake the mixture in a muffin tin lined with paper cake cases instead

This simple drizzled seed cake is a kitchen-witch recipe for helping to rebalance overworked emotions. It's an ideal treat for anyone who's upset, angry, or having trouble with insomnia or intrusive thoughts. Poppy seed calms the body and soul, soothes heartbreak, and promotes tranquillity while imparting a subtle nutty, spiced taste. Chamomile aids restful sleep and alleviates tension with its gentle floral sweetness. Both work with mood-elevating lemon to create a lovely comfort-food flavour reminiscent of carefree summer days. All of the ingredients can be found in supermarkets and keep well at home, so it's an easy recipe to make at any time. Share it with friends who need the healing power of a good chat over tea and cake, or treat yourself to a slice whenever family life, work or hormones are threatening to make you feel frazzled.

Start by making a simple lemon syrup by boiling together the water, lemon juice and caster sugar. When the syrup has reduced slightly, turn off the heat and add the chamomile tea bags. Try to use pure chamomile tea rather than a fruit blend, which may contain liquorice that can interfere with other herbs and with medication. Leave to steep for 20 minutes then remove the chamomile tea bags, stir and allow to cool. Any syrup left over at the end of the recipe can be stored in a sealed jar or plastic container and will keep in the fridge for around two weeks.

Cream together the butter and caster sugar. Add the lemon curd then beat in the 3 eggs. Add the flour and fold in until the cake mix drops off of a spoon when lifted and turned. If you need to add more liquid to get a dropping texture, use a couple of drops of either milk or the chamomile syrup. Stir in the lemon zest and poppy seeds.

Line a loaf tin or 20cm cake tin with greaseproof paper and pour in the cake mix. Bake at Gas Mark 3/170°C/325°F for approximately 45-50 minutes. A knife or skewer inserted into the middle of the cake will come away clean when it is done.

Take the cake out of the tin and put on a wire rack to cool. When it's almost cold, prick it all over with a skewer, cocktail stick or fork. Brush a little of the chamomile syrup over the top.

Make a drizzle from the icing sugar and chamomile syrup, adding the liquid slowly until you create a thick, viscous liquid, and drizzle this over the cake. Leave to cool entirely before serving. Garnish the iced cake with lemon zest and chamomile flowers.

> *Share it with friends who need the healing power of a good chat over tea and cake*

CALM-DOWN CAKE

Lemon has a bright, mood-elevating flavour and when combined with the sweetness of sugar it represents happiness

Chamomile and poppy seed are both calming ingredients that help to soothe and rebalance emotions

You'll Need...

For the cake mix

- 8 oz / 227g self-raising flour
- 7 oz / 198g caster sugar
- 6 oz / 1.5 sticks / 170g unsalted butter
- 3 eggs
- 1 tbsp lemon curd
- Zest of 1 unwaxed lemon
- 1 oz / 28g poppy seeds

For the chamomile syrup

- 2.5 fl oz / ⅓ cup / 75ml water
- 2.5 fl oz / ⅓ cup / 75ml lemon juice
- 10.5 oz / 300g caster sugar
- 2 chamomile teabags

For the chamomile drizzle

- 1-2 tbsp chamomile syrup
- 3 oz / 85g icing sugar

To garnish

- Lemon zest
- Fresh or dried chamomile flowers (optional)

GREEN WITCHCRAFT

Go Crazy *for* Crystals

CRYSTALS ARE RENOWNED FOR THEIR METAPHYSICAL PROPERTIES AND THEY CAN BE AN INVALUABLE TOOL FOR DIVINATION, BOTH IN THEIR OWN RIGHT AND IN CONJUNCTION WITH OTHER METHODS

WORDS Alice Pattillo

Crystals and stones have enchanted and intrigued mankind for millennia, their beauty revered and their magic put to use as jewels, charms and protective talismans. They've been used to form monuments like stone circles and temples, carved into relics and employed for meditation, magic and soothsaying. The act of divination with stones, precious, semi-precious or otherwise, is known as lithomancy. There are three common types of lithomancy: stone casting or throwing, crystallomancy and dowsing.

Casting or throwing stones is a form of sortilege and the method most commonly associated with the term lithomancy. This process involves the caster tossing tumbled stones like dice and interpreting where they fall in relation to each other, as well as the patterns they form.

Crystallomancy is the most prominent form of lithomancy and refers to divination performed in the form of gazing at a reflective stone, often a polished gemstone, and methods involve using the crystal as a meditative focal point or scrying. This is perfect for those new to crystals.

Gemstones are also often used as a tool in dowsing. In fact, crystal dowsing is perhaps the most prevalent modern form of dowsing. They are said to be a useful source of magical energy, aiding intuition and clairvoyance. Simply incorporate them into your everyday life via jewellery, or place them upon your altar and allow their metaphysical properties to elevate your practice.

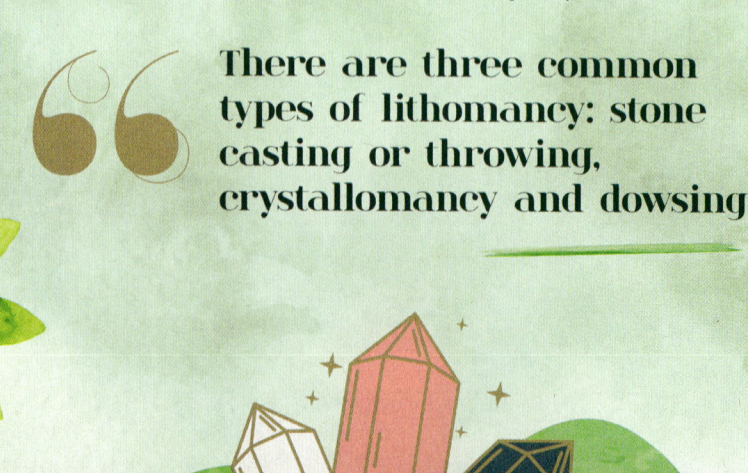

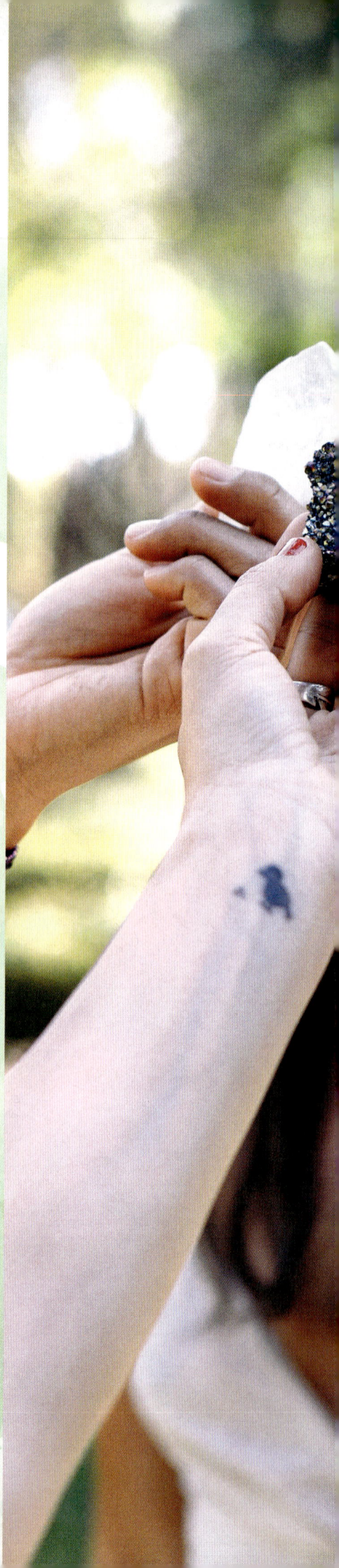

> There are three common types of lithomancy: stone casting or throwing, crystallomancy and dowsing

GO CRAZY FOR CRYSYALS

Predicting with Pendulums

Crystal pendulums are commonly used for divination in the form of dowsing

Traditionally, pendulum dowsing was used to locate water, minerals and other valuable objects hidden beneath the ground, but dowsing with crystals can reveal much more than just a hidden hot spring. Crystal pendulums are useful for quick decision making and to enhance other divination techniques. Try using it in conjunction with the tarot to help pick out and interpret the cards. Pendulums can also be used to diagnose possible health issues. Try using one on a friend to scan their whole body to reveal energy blockages and internal issues.

DID YOU KNOW...
You can make your own crystal pendulum with a gemstone bead, point or charm, and some thread

Scry Your Heart Out

Crystal gazing is one of the oldest and most popular forms of fortune-telling

Crystal gazing is a form of scrying, peering into a reflective gemstone and reading the shapes found inside the stone, or interpreting reflections bouncing off of its surface. While scrying can be performed on almost anything reflective, it is most popularly practised with a crystal ball. The ball should be perfectly spherical (without a flattened base) and may be fashioned out of quartz, obsidian, beryl, calcite or even lead crystal (glass). If glass, the ball should be perfectly clear, with no air bubbles. A transparent or translucent ball allows the gazer to interpret refracted light through it. Natural crystals may contain shapes formed within its natural structure or inclusions of other minerals, which can then be interpreted. You could get started with a simple crystal tumblestone, though.

Images Getty Images

GREEN WITCHCRAFT

Fall In Love with Lithomancy

This method of crystal fortune-telling is all about listening to your gut

Lithomancy, or stone casting, is an incredibly simple yet highly effective and insightful form of fortune telling. Stone casting involves throwing a collection of stones, held in the palm of your hand or within a small bag. It can be performed with a large number of crystals (in which case you will need a small bag) or just a few. You can toss them onto a table, the floor or even into water and interpret the ripples they create. You may also like to pay attention to the light refractions and reflections created if you are using polished or transparent stones. You needn't spend a penny on a fancy kit, you can use any crystals you may already have – your favourite clear quartz pendant, an amethyst ring or a pair of rose quartz earrings will work perfectly – although picking out a few tumblestones from your local metaphysical store is a therapeutic process, and will allow you to choose crystals that have qualities you are seeking. You'll want a set of at least ten crystals that you're familiar with in terms of each of the stone's meanings and properties, as this will aid you in interpreting meaning. But, the most important aspect of reading the stones is to use your intuition. As with all divination, it can be useful to cleanse your space with incense beforehand and always cleanse your crystals afterwards, using water or smoke.

DID YOU KNOW…

Plain white or clear quartz is one of the most powerful crystals, sometimes called the Master Healer

GO CRAZY FOR CRYSYALS

Casting Stones for Love

1 Set up your circle

You may want to draw a circle using chalk or tape, lay out a cloth, use a pendulum or crystal grid or set up a space on a table. A mat or grid, particularly one that has an astrological or seasonal wheel printed onto it, will aid in your interpretation. With your eyes closed, intuitively select three crystals from your set (you may want to reach into a bag for this!) and hold them in the palm of your dominant hand.

2 Ask a question

Focus on a question, the answer of which should take into account three perspectives: your feelings, your partner's point of view and the situation. Something like "is my relationship heading for marriage?" or "is there a chance we will get back together?". Once you have decided on your question, ask it to the stones, focus and meditate on it and as you do, release your stones all at once into the circle or designated space.

3 Trust your intuition

Pay attention to where each crystal lands. The crystal that lands closest to you represents you – your motivation and true feelings. The stone central to the space or circle is the action to be taken. The third stone, neither central nor near you, represents your partner's feelings. Notice what crystals lay where – their properties and meanings. Consider where they have fallen in relation to each other and within your space, and if there are any reflections or light refractions casting off them. Pick up each one individually and get a feel for them. Does anything come immediately to mind when you touch each one? Go with your gut feeling!

A cloth or mat with an astrological or wheel of the year guide can help with interpreting meanings

GREEN WITCHCRAFT

How Crystals Work

WHAT CAN CRYSTALS DO FOR US?
QUITE A LOT, AS IT TURNS OUT…

WORDS April Madden

You do crystal magic every day without even realising it. When you wake up and turn your phone alarm off, you touch a screen that has a Liquid Crystal Display (LCD). Your touch sends an electrical signal to the phone's interface that tells it to do something, whether that's turning your alarm off, checking your What'sApp or opening TikTok. The liquid crystals in screens change colour when light is passed through them; by organising that light and the crystals it shines through, your phone shows you the app you want. The same technology powers your TV and the screens you see everywhere in everyday life. Or maybe you've printed something out recently? Inside each cartridge of printer ink there's a tiny crystal that responds to subsonic electrical vibrations called piezoelectrics. When you tell the printer to print, it sends an electrical pulse through those crystals and makes them vibrate, releasing a bubble of ink onto the paper. Crystals are also highly sensitive to radio frequencies and can pick them out of the air; in the early days of broadcasting a simple device made of crystal and metal inside a radio enabled you to listen to music over the airwaves. Silicon crystal semiconductors are at the heart of today's phones and computers, and scientists have experimented with using a type of fused quartz to store vast quantities of information and access it more quickly than current technology can. The power of crystals is all around you, in constant use by ordinary, everyday devices.

Quartz is one of the most common and useful crystals. Made up of silicon and oxygen, it's the world's second-most common mineral (the first is feldspar, a group that contains beautiful crystals such as moonstone and labradorite). There are many different types of quartz to be found – amethyst, carnelian, agate, tiger's eye, aventurine and citrine are all

Grow your own

You can grow your own crystals in a cleaned-out jam jar using a relatively inexpensive kit, available from retailers including toy stores, science museums and Amazon. You won't be able to grow anything you can wear or use, but it's a fun experiment in seeing how crystals are formed!

You can grow single crystals in a jar, or 'crystal gardens' like these ones, using a simple kit you can buy online

HOW CRYSTALS WORK

quartzes. Like all crystals, their colour and properties are influenced by the elements in their crystalline makeup. As well as silicon and oxygen, citrine contains iron, which gives it its orange-yellow hue. Iron can also be responsible for amethyst's purple and rose quartz's pink.

Quartzes are used in clocks and watches and have piezoelectric properties, so they often also turn up in printers. They can be custom-grown in a lab as well as found naturally. But they have more esoteric uses as well. Rose quartz is famous for its beautifying properties, making it a common material for use in massage tools, particularly facial rollers and gua sha stones.

It's their sensitivity to intangible vibrations, combined with crystals' ability to receive, modulate, store and broadcast that makes proponents of crystals believe in their more arcane powers. Former scientist Rupert Sheldrake, now a parapsychology researcher and author, proposed a theory called 'morphic resonance' in which he stated his belief that natural systems – crystals among them – inherited and stored memories from others of their kind. One common example is growing successive crystal gardens in the same jar, and how they can follow the same pattern of growth as the previous layout, even when the jar has been sterilised and the starter chemicals are arranged differently. Sheldrake's theory was dismissed as pseudo-science and he was censured by the scientific community, and sceptics maintain that the only effect crystals produce in humans is a placebo – they only have an effect because we believe that they will. Many of the things that crystal proponents believe that crystals interact with – such as auras – are also considered pseudo-scientific, meaning there's little possibility of any definitive research proving (or disproving) those beliefs. Many of us, however, find we're drawn to particular kinds of crystals. Whether that's simply an aesthetic attraction or an affinity on a deeper level may never be definitively proven.

> **In the early days of broadcasting, a device made of crystal and metal inside a radio enabled you to listen to music over the airwaves**

Crystals captivate us with their beauty, but they're far more useful than mere adornment

GREEN WITCHCRAFT

The Magic of Crystals

DEVOTEES BELIEVE ALL CRYSTALS HAVE MAGICAL PROPERTIES, BUT WHICH ARE THE ONES THAT CAN AMP UP RITUALS AND SPELLS?

WORDS April Madden

All crystals are believed to have magical properties. Practitioners of magic use what are called correspondences to find the right crystal to use in their ritual or spell. Correspondences are lists and tables that can include crystals, colours, plants, planets and much more; they're designed to help practitioners find the right tools for building a spell. They take into account an object's properties, colour, mythological associations and more. Rose quartz, for example, with its pink colouration, gentle vibrational energy, and traditional link to Venus, is considered a perfect ingredient for romantic love spells. But for a love spell that wanted to invoke passion instead, fiery, strengthening carnelian, with its link to the sexy sacral chakra, would be a better bet.

While most spells and rituals that involve crystals rely on the practitioner getting the right tool for the job, there are some stones that help with

Top 5 Crystals for Spellwork

Whether you want to dive straight into crystal magic, or you're already a magic worker who wants to introduce crystals to their practice, here are five essential stones to help with your spells

BLACK TOURMALINE
Black stones help to protect the spellcaster from negative energies. Try onyx or obsidian if tourmaline is out of your price range.

MOONSTONE
Tap into the magic of the moon with its sacred stone. Rainbow moonstone is actually white labradorite, giving you the benefits of both stones.

LABRADORITE
Think of it as the equivalent of sticking an antenna on your spellcraft – mystical labradorite offers your magic a signal boost. It's beautiful, too.

CLEAR QUARTZ
This do-everything stone is a great all-rounder, perfect for anyone just starting to use crystals in their spells. It's also inexpensive and easy to get hold of.

AVENTURINE
Green stones help nature witches attune to the power of the Earth. Jade, green onyx, malachite and chrysoprase are also good options.

THE MAGIC OF CRYSTALS

magic itself, whatever its aim may be. Most spellcasters will begin their ritual by surrounding themselves with a physical and psychic circle of water, salt, and energy. Ritual magic can be a dangerous business, though; stones like onyx, obsidian and black tourmaline have powerful protective properties to help guard the would-be magician from negative energies. They could be placed at the four cardinal points of the circle or worn as a protective talisman.

Labradorite is an interesting specimen of feldspar that was first scientifically identified in Canada's Labrador region in 1770. It had long been known to the Indigenous people of the land, however. Labradorite can appear dull greeny-grey until the light hits it, when it displays its unique property of labradorescence and shimmers with an unearthly, spectral blue glow. To Labrador's Indigenous population, this was the wild elemental sorcery of the Northern Lights, fallen to the cold earth and frozen into stone. Magical practitioners believe that labradorite's unique property makes it a powerful amplifier of magic, and that it can be used to enhance and boost one's own magical gifts.

Another incredibly magical stone is far more common. Clear quartz, referred to by some practitioners as the Master Healer, is also a strong amplifier. Believed to enhance creativity, wisdom and the ability to learn, as well as being associated with light and healing, it's the ideal stone for anyone wanting to get started with the magic of crystals and for anyone who feels they need a bit of a boost.

Tap into Your Third Eye

Many magical traditions have an awareness of the third eye, the intuitive sense that some believe allows us to see hidden things or scry the future. In ancient Hindu teachings, the third eye is one of seven chakras, or energy points, and the wise use of the right crystals can enhance its abilities. Try meditating with a smooth fluorite tumblestone to balance and enhance your third eye. Start by sitting and holding it, letting your physical eyes wander over and through the stone's shifting colours, and relax into contemplating them. After a couple of meditation sessions like this, try lying down with your eyes closed and placing the same stone between your brows, visualising the colour play you've previously observed in your mind and imagining your fluorite crystal as a lens that your third eye can gaze through.

> There are some stones that help with magic itself, whatever its aim may be

DID YOU KNOW...
Practitioners of magic believe that crystals can offer them protection, enhance their metaphysical abilities, and help them connect to the elements

GREEN WITCHCRAFT

Grow your Garden with a Gemstone Grid

ENHANCE EARTH ENERGY AND BOOST THE GROWTH
AND HEALTH OF YOUR PLANTS WITH THIS EASY
GRID TO ATTRACT ABUNDANCE TO YOUR GARDEN,
GREENHOUSE OR EVEN HOUSE PLANTS

WORDS Alice Pattillo

Nurturing plants can be a difficult task. Understanding your plants' needs can be tough. Many plants seem temperamental – if everything isn't 'just right' you might find your foliage failing and by the time you discover they are struggling, it is often too late. In order to help your herbs, facilitate your flowers and revitalise your vegetation, consider utilising Mother Nature's transcendent toolkit: crystals! Crystals speak the language of each of nature's elements and can inject life into your failing garden or perishing potted plants.

Firstly, find suitable crystals that'll satisfy your plant's needs. Crystals in their raw state are best for potent earth energy, but some can be too delicate to keep outside, so tumbled stones, polished points and pyramids are all perfect for manifesting and attracting abundance.

Green-coloured stones are excellent for healing, nurturing and harnessing natural power. Browny-red hues are grounding yet reproductively stimulating crystals. For dull climates or plants struggling in the shade, add some orange and yellow hues. A chunk of clear quartz never goes amiss, either – the Master Healer reportedly helps tomato plants resist pests.

Once you've amassed a small selection of stones – in numerology, eight is the number of prosperity and victory so we are working with eight! – you will want to cleanse your crystals (you can do this by simply running them under the tap) and charge them by laying them out in the sun for an hour or two. Next comes the gridding. We will be creating a spiral shape, spinning clockwise to symbolise the sun, the cycle of life, nature and the seasons to encourage growth. Decide where your grid will be placed – somewhere central in your garden or at the base of the plant or the centre of the area where you want to stimulate

Moss agate is known as the Gardener's Stone thanks to its potent earth energies

GEMSTONE GRID

> *Green-coloured stones are excellent for healing, nurturing and harnessing natural power*

The spiral is a symbol of growth and creation and can be found inscribed into stone artefacts left by ancient cultures all over the world in various forms

From left to right: clear quartz helps amplify other crystal energies, while pyrite invigorates with strong solar energies and sodalite is full of creativity

You'll Need...

Eight crystals in raw, tumbled or polished form

- **MOSS AGATE** The Gardener's Stone for healing (can be substituted with tree agate)
- **GREEN AVENTURINE** For thriving plant life
- **MALACHITE** For strength, connection and fertility
- **GREEN CALCITE** For luck, prosperity and health
- **ARAGONITE** A potent earth healer attuned to Mother Earth
- **PYRITE** For protection, strength and solar energy (can be substituted with tiger's eye, or hematite if your plants require less solar power)
- **CITRINE** For protection, abundance, creativity and solar energy (it can be substituted with yellow calcite)
- **CLEAR QUARTZ** The Master Healer reportedly helps resist pests and disease

the most growth, preferably not in direct sunlight. Once charged, start to arrange the crystals in a spiral shape in your selected area or plant pot. Begin with a central crystal and move circularly outwards in a clockwise direction. As you place each stone, recite the following:

"I commit these crystals back to the earth and invoke Mother Nature for nurture and rebirth".

You might want to leave the grid out permanently (if you are working in the garden, you will need to ensure it is in a protected place, shielded from the elements) or remove the grid after a week and repeat the spell.

The Essential Guide to
Green Witchcraft

Future PLC Quay House, The Ambury, Bath, BA1 1UA

Editorial
Editor **April Madden**
Art Editor **Thomas Parrett**
Head of Art & Design **Greg Whitaker**
Editorial Director **Jon White**
Managing Director **Grainne McKenna**

Contributors
Peg Aloi, Catherine Curzon, Andy Downes, Ben Gazur, Harriet Knight,
Jessica Leggett, Alice Pattillo, Drew Sleep, Katy Stokes,
Poppy-Jay St Palmer, Sally Trotman & Willow Winsham

Cover images
Shutterstock, Getty Images

Photography
All copyrights and trademarks are recognised and respected

Advertising
Media packs are available on request
Commercial Director **Clare Dove**

International
Head of Print Licensing **Rachel Shaw**
licensing@futurenet.com
www.futurecontenthub.com

Circulation
Head of Newstrade **Tim Mathers**

Production
Head of Production **Mark Constance**
Production Project Manager **Matthew Eglinton**
Advertising Production Manager **Joanne Crosby**
Digital Editions Controller **Jason Hudson**
Production Managers **Keely Miller, Nola Cokely,
Vivienne Calvert, Fran Twentyman**

Printed in the UK

Distributed by Marketforce, 5 Churchill Place, Canary Wharf, London, E14 5HU
www.marketforce.co.uk – For enquiries, please email:
mfcommunications@futurenet.com

The Essential Guide to Green Witchcraft First Edition (LBZ5496)
© 2023 Future Publishing Limited

We are committed to only using magazine paper which is derived from responsibly managed,
certified forestry and chlorine-free manufacture. The paper in this bookazine was sourced
and produced from sustainable managed forests, conforming to strict environmental and
socioeconomic standards.

All contents © 2023 Future Publishing Limited or published under licence. All rights reserved.
No part of this magazine may be used, stored, transmitted or reproduced in any way without
the prior written permission of the publisher. Future Publishing Limited (company number
2008885) is registered in England and Wales. Registered office: Quay House, The Ambury, Bath
BA1 1UA. All information contained in this publication is for information only and is, as far as
we are aware, correct at the time of going to press. Future cannot accept any responsibility
for errors or inaccuracies in such information. You are advised to contact manufacturers and
retailers directly with regard to the price of products/services referred to in this publication.
Apps and websites mentioned in this publication are not under our control. We are not
responsible for their contents or any other changes or updates to them. This magazine is fully
independent and not affiliated in any way with the companies mentioned herein.

FUTURE
Connectors.
Creators.
Experience
Makers.

Future plc is a public
company quoted on the
London Stock Exchange
(symbol: FUTR)
www.futureplc.com

Chief Executive Officer **Jon Steinberg**
Non-Executive Chairman **Richard Huntingford**
Chief Financial and Strategy Officer **Penny Ladkin-Brand**

Tel +44 (0)1225 442 244

Widely Recycled

ipso. For press freedom
with responsibility